Paul's Epistle to the Galatians

Paul's Epistle
to the Galatians

Only One Gospel

Erwin R. Gane

ORION
PUBLISHING
Ukiah, CA

P.O. Box 449
Ukiah, CA 95482
800-471-4284

ISBN 0-9744082-0-4

Cover Design by Haley Trimmer, Amazing Facts

Contents

Chapter 1
How to Unite a Divided Church

Acts 1, 8-11, 13-15

What should a church do when divisions arise? When members in the local church espouse contradictory beliefs or conflicting lifestyles, what should be done about it? Suppose the conflict becomes more widespread, with many churches or even the worldwide church involved; what action should be taken by the leadership to restore harmony of belief and practice?

Some people would urge that a controversial subject, whatever it might be, should be avoided. They believe that if church members would simply refuse to discuss the issue the problem would go away.

What did Jesus do when He was accused of creating division among the Jews? John records that "there was a division among the people because of him" (John 7:43). "There was a division therefore again among the Jews for these sayings. And many of them said, He hath a devil, and is mad; why hear ye him? Others said, These are not the words of him that hath a devil" (John 10:19-21). Did Jesus change His message because it was divisive? On the contrary, He continued to proclaim it with loving, earnest enthusiasm.

Does this mean that anyone in the church today, who is convinced that he has a message that others do not have, has a mandate to propagate his point of view in the church, even

7

though leaders and members have serious doubts about the truth of his teaching? Indeed, no! Jesus was God, as well as man. His teaching was divine, absolute truth. Would anyone dare to harbor the presumption that his or her personal views on religious issues have the same unquestionable authority as the teachings of Jesus?

But suppose the divisive point of view is the teaching of Jesus. Suppose the person espousing and proclaiming a message in the church is convinced, and others are convinced, that he has clear scriptural support for his position, even though there are many who reject it. What attitude should that individual take to the church, and specifically to those in the church who oppose the message? Should that person assume that, because he is the "wheat" and his opponents are the "tares," he should dissociate himself from his apostate brethren and sisters?

How would Jesus answer that question? He taught: "Let both grow together until the harvest" (Matthew 13:30). The individual who separates from the church because his brethren and sisters do not see light in his teaching is acting directly contrary to Jesus' instruction. He is not uprooting the tares from the church; he is uprooting the wheat. He as the wheat is refusing to associate with the tares, and this is contrary to Jesus' instruction. However truthful his message might be, his attitude to his brethren and sisters in the church is not Christian.

The Issue Faced by Paul

The apostle Paul was thoroughly convinced that his teaching was divinely revealed Christian truth. His opponents in Syrian Antioch and Galatia were equally convinced that they had the truth.

What were the options open to Paul? He could have slugged it out with his theological opponents, refusing to be concerned about the resulting division in the church. He could have separated from the apostolic church, taking with him those loyal followers who believed his message. One simple solution might have been for Paul to change the subject. He might have turned his attention to prophetic interpretation, or the ethical message of the Old Testament prophets, or the comforting passages of the Psalms. Why didn't he simply leave the issue alone for a while? A moratorium on discussion of the controversial subject might have resulted in a gradual restoration of peace and harmony.

Paul gave a remarkable example of how teachers of controversial issues should act. At the end of his first missionary journey (about A.D. 47), he returned with Barnabas, to Syrian Antioch (see Acts 14:26-28). "Certain men which came down from Judaea taught the brethren, and said, Except ye be circumcised after the manner of Moses, ye cannot be saved" (Acts 15:1). Now that was no small assertion. These Jewish Christians from Jerusalem were teaching Gentiles that they could not be Christians and could not enjoy salvation unless they practiced circumcision and laws of that kind.

Paul objected strenuously. As you read the account you can almost hear him arguing with them. The issue was not some peripheral matter that had no genuine relevance to the heart of the gospel message. In the final analysis, the issue was, What is the gospel, and how is a person saved?

The party of Jewish Christians from Jerusalem were saying that there are some laws that have to be obeyed strictly in order for you to be saved. One of those laws was Moses' command regarding circumcision. Paul said, No. You are wrong. Circumcision is no longer required as a religious practice because it met its fulfillment when Jesus died and rose again. Outward circumcision symbolized transformation of heart (see Deuteronomy 10:16; 30:6). The death and resurrection of Jesus made possible this transformation by the converting work of the Holy Spirit. The experience to which circumcision pointed met its fulfillment in Christ's work for the one who accepts His sacrifice (see Romans 2:28, 29; Galatians 6:15; Ephesians 2:11-13). Type is now replaced by antitype, example is invalidated by reality, shadow is dispelled by the full blaze of gospel glory.

Paul did not stop there. He saw a much deeper issue. If circumcision is essential to salvation, he urged, then there is something we can do to save ourselves. In fact, Paul taught, salvation does not result from obedience to any law—moral, ceremonial, or civil. Salvation is by God's grace alone, "without the law" (Romans 3:21), "not of works, lest any man should boast" (Ephesians 2:9).

Ah, replied his opponents, now we see where you are going. You are an antinomian. You are opposed to all of God's law. You don't believe that any of God's laws should be kept.

Not so, Paul replied. I believe that obedience to God's moral law of ten commandments is an essential result of the saving experience. But the ceremonial laws that pointed forward to the work of Jesus Christ have now ceased to be binding upon Christian believers.

Paul's point was simply that, although we are not saved by obedience to any law, such obedience is the natural result of the saving work of God's grace in the heart. He could have quoted Jesus for that: " 'If you love me, you will obey what I command' " (John 14:15, NIV). Throughout his ministry Paul constantly upheld the moral law of ten commandments as Christ's standard of righteousness. "Do we, then, nullify the law by this faith? Not at all! Rather, we uphold the law" (Romans 3:31, NIV). The grace of Christ saves us when we have faith. The result is that the law of God is established in our hearts.

"What shall we say, then," Paul wrote. "Is the law sin? Certainly not! Indeed I would not have known what sin was except through the law. For I would not have known what it was to covet if the law had not said, 'Do not covet' "(Romans 7:7, NIV). You see, the Ten Commandments for Paul still functioned, not as a means of salvation, but as a standard of righteousness. They pointed out sin in his life. Christ's cleansing grace is the answer to the sin problem; cleansing grace that brings our lives into agreement with the principles of His holy law.

Just why did Christ die, Paul asked. His answer totally refuted the accusations of his opponents. Christ died "in order that the righteous requirements of the law might be fully met in us, who do not live according to the sinful nature but according to the Spirit" (Romans 8:4, NIV). Salvation does not come by obedience to any law. But the person who enjoys present salvation in Christ is in harmony with the moral principles of the Ten Commandments.

The Action Paul Took

The legalistic Jewish Christians from Jerusalem were not convinced by Paul's explanations. They persisted in demanding that Gentile converts be circumcised and keep the other aspects of the ceremonial law. They were convinced that if Paul's teaching prevailed the whole fabric of Judaism would come apart at the seams. The ancient sanctuary services were still very much alive in their minds. The Jews as a nation had rejected Jesus Christ as the Messiah, yet they continued to offer their animal sacrifices and continued to observe their annual ceremonial feast days as types of the work of the coming Messiah.

The legalistic Jewish Christians could not grasp that the ceremonial aspects of the law were a temporary foreshadowing of the sacrificial, mediatorial, and judgment ministry of the Messiah. Paul tried to explain that the Messiah made these temporary observances obsolete. Again and again throughout his ministry Paul and other apostles stressed the same truth (see Ephesians 2:11-17; Hebrews 7-10).

Paul could see that he was getting nowhere with the Jewish legalists in Syrian Antioch. Following the direction of the local church, he and Barnabas went to Jerusalem to counsel with the world leaders (see Acts 15:2-4). How significant it is that local church members were willing to seek wider counsel on the issues that divided them! How significant it is that the apostle Paul, convinced that his message came directly from Christ, was willing to follow the direction of the local church that he should counsel with the leading apostles in Jerusalem!

How many today, of those whose messages have thrilled large numbers of people, would be willing to submit their teachings to the scrutiny of the church's leaders from various parts of the world field? Thank the Lord, throughout the history of the church, leaders such as Paul have done precisely that.

Leaders today are not apostles in the sense that the early Christian leaders were, but the Lord has invested them with the responsibility to study, pray, and counsel with their brethren. There is wisdom in many counselors and great wisdom in the policy of sharing with experienced minds one's discoveries in the Word of God.

"By some, all efforts to establish order are regarded as dangerous—as a restriction of personal liberty, and hence to be feared as popery. These deceived souls regard it a virtue to boast of their freedom to think and act independently. They declare that they will not take any man's say-so, that they are amenable to no man. I have been instructed that it is Satan's special effort to lead men to feel that God is pleased to have them choose their own course independent of the counsel of their brethren. . . .

"Some have advanced the thought that, as we near the close of time, every child of God will act independently of any religious organization. But I have been instructed by the Lord that in this work there is no such thing as every man's being independent. The stars of heaven are all under law, each influencing the other to do the will of God, yielding their common obedience to the law that controls their action. And, in order that the Lord's work may advance healthfully and solidly, His people must draw together. . . .

"I have often been instructed by the Lord that no man's judgment should be surrendered to the judgment of any other one man. Never should the mind of one man or the minds of a few men be regarded as sufficient in wisdom and power to control the work and to say what plans shall be followed. But when, in a General Conference, the judgment of the brethren assembled from all parts of the field is exercised, private independence and private judgment must not be stubbornly maintained, but surrendered. Never should a laborer regard as a virtue the persistent maintenance of his position of independence, contrary to the decision of the general body" (*Testimonies*, vol. 9, pp. 257-260).

The Decision of the Jerusalem Council

The Jerusalem Council described in Acts 15 is thought to have met about A.D. 49. The council discussed in detail the issue troubling the church of Antioch. Paul made a comprehensive presentation of the gospel he was preaching among the Gentiles. Both Peter and James then endorsed his approach. The general council voted to send the following message to the believers in Antioch: "It seemed good to the Holy Spirit and to us not to burden you with anything beyond the following requirements: You are to abstain from food sacrificed to idols, from blood, from the meat of strangled animals and from sexual immorality. You will do well to avoid these things" (Acts 15:28, 29, NIV).

Paul's message was upheld. It was not necessary for Gentile Christians to receive circumcision or involve themselves in the ceremonies of the Jewish sanctuary service.

The Controversy Today

Some contemporary Christians use the decisions of the Jerusalem Council to support a belief as extreme as that of the legalistic Jews of Paul's day. Their argument is that the brethren at the Jerusalem Council effectively abolished the Ten Commandments. They say that the apostles held that the "law of Moses" need no longer be kept (see Acts 15:5, 24). The "law of Moses," they teach, includes both the moral law of ten commandments and the ceremonial laws. Therefore if you reject the "law of Moses," as the apostles did, you reject the Ten Commandments.

Some interpreters have tried to answer this argument by emphasizing that the law of Moses included only the ceremonial laws. The law of God, they say, is the Ten Commandments. This position is not defensible from Scripture. There can be no doubt that the law of Moses included the Ten Commandments. Moses completed the writing of the book of the law toward the end of his life (see Deuteronomy 31:9, 24-26). This book of the law, which included the Ten Commandments, was placed beside the ark in the tabernacle. The only law placed inside the ark of the covenant was that written on the tables of stone (see 1 Kings 8:9). But the same Ten Commandments were included in the book of the law that was placed beside the ark (see Deuteronomy 30:10; 33:2-4; 1 Kings

2:3). Nehemiah, for example, made no distinction between "the book of the law of Moses" and "the book of the law of God" (see Nehemiah 8, 9, 10).

Jesus included the Ten Commandments in the law of Moses (see Mark 7:10; John 7:19-23). The epistle to the Hebrews reminds us that "anyone who rejected the law of Moses died without mercy on the testimony of two or three witnesses" (Hebrews 10:28, NIV). Yet we know that the death penalty according to the law of Moses was meted out especially for transgression of one of the Ten Commandments (see Deuteronomy 13:6, 10; 21:18, 21; 22:20-27).

The point is that "the law of Moses" is a general term for all the laws contained in the Pentateuch (the five books of Moses), including the Ten Commandments. When applied specifically to particular laws, it must be determined from the context whether the phrase "the law of Moses" refers to ceremonial laws, civil laws, or the Ten Commandments. In Luke 2:22, "the law of Moses" refers to the ceremonial law. In Hebrews 10:26-29, "the law of Moses" means especially the Ten Commandments.

Acts chapter 15 deals with circumcision and laws of that kind. The part of the law of Moses not commanded by the apostles, therefore, includes laws of that type. Those who think that the council described in Acts 15 abolished the Ten Commandments should be willing to accept the instruction of the apostles who were present. They consistently upheld the Ten Commandments as the continuing standard of righteousness for Christians who are saved by grace alone (see Romans 3:31; 7:7, 12, 14; 8:3, 4; James 2:10-12; 1 John 2:4; Revelation 12:17; 14:12).

Summary

Confronted by serious controversy in the church of Antioch, the apostle Paul willingly accepted the direction of the local church and consulted with the apostles in Jerusalem.

By accepting the decisions of the assembled general conference of the church in regard to belief and Christian practice we conform to Christ's will as made known to the church by the Holy Spirit. He is the divine Interpreter of His Word (John 16:13), the ultimate Possessor and Dispenser of the Keys of the Kingdom of heaven (see Matthew 16:19; 18:18; Revelation 1:18).

Chapter 2
How Not to Be Right With God

Galatians 1

Soon after the Jerusalem Council (A.D. 49) Paul set out on his second missionary journey. This journey, described in Acts 15:36—18:22, occupied the years from approximately A.D. 49 to 52. Accompanied by Silas, Paul traveled overland, first north and then west from Syrian Antioch visiting the churches in the southern part of the Roman province of Galatia. Paul had established churches in the cities of this region on his first missionary journey: Derbe, Lystra, Iconium, and Antioch. On this second visit his great concern was to foster the spiritual life of the believers and announce to them the decisions of the Jerusalem Council (see Acts 16:4, 5).

Continuing his journey, Paul traveled farther north "throughout Phrygia and the region of Galatia" (Acts 16:6). At that time there lived in central and northern Asia Minor a people known as Gauls or Galatians. They had established the cities of Tavium, Ancyra, and Pessinus. The Roman province of Galatia included the territory inhabited by these people, as well as the cities of the south whose people were not Galatians by blood descent.

Scholars argue about whether the epistle of Paul to the Galatians was written to the churches in the southern part of the Roman province of Galatia or to those in the north. However, it is not necessary to know which group Paul was addressing to understand the message of the letter. There is ample evidence that Paul wrote to the north Galatian churches he had established on his second missionary journey.

After describing the visit to the churches in the south, where the people were well known to Paul, Luke simply states: "Now when they had gone throughout Phrygia and the region of Galatia" (Acts 16:6). Thus he distinguished between the southern region and the territory of Galatia.

"Having visited the churches in Pisidia and the neighboring region, Paul and Silas, with Timothy, pressed on into 'Phrygia and the region of Galatia,' where with mighty power they proclaimed the glad tidings of salvation. The Galatians were given up to the worship of idols; but, as the apostles preached to them, they rejoiced in the message that promised freedom from the thralldom of sin. Paul and his fellow workers proclaimed the doctrine of righteousness by faith in the atoning sacrifice of Christ. They presented Christ as the one who, seeing the helpless condition of the fallen race, came to redeem men and women by living a life of obedience to God's law and by paying the penalty of disobedience. And in the light of the cross many who had never before known of the true God, began to comprehend the greatness of the Father's love" (*The Acts of the Apostles*, pp. 207, 208).

Evidently Paul first visited the Galatians because he was in need of rest and recuperation. "You know it was because of a bodily ailment that I preached the gospel to you at first; and though my condition was a trial to you, you did not scorn or despise me, but received me as an angel of God, as Christ Jesus. What has become of the satisfaction you felt? For I bear you witness that, if possible, you would have plucked out your eyes and given them to me" (Galatians 4:13-15, RSV). "Paul had a bodily affliction; his eyesight was bad. He thought that by earnest prayer the difficulty might be removed. But the Lord had His own purpose, and He said to Paul, Speak to Me no more of this matter. My grace is sufficient. It will enable you to bear the infirmity" (*SDA Bible Commentary*, vol. 6, p. 1107; compare 2 Cor. 12:7-10).

At the end of the second missionary journey, Paul and his

associates returned to Antioch in Syria. "After spending some time there he departed and went from place to place through the region of Galatia and Phrygia, strengthening all the disciples" (Acts 18:23, RSV). A good pastor, Paul was not satisfied to win souls to Christ and then ignore them. His concern was that those who had found the way of salvation by faith should grow spiritually, ever coming nearer to the Lord, daily gaining from Christ the strength to meet the difficulties and trials of life. This is why he visited the Galatians again on the third missionary journey. He was deeply concerned for their spiritual welfare.

Toward the end of the third missionary journey, Paul visited Corinth in Greece. "There he spent three months" (Acts 20:3, RSV). Many scholars have thought that it was during that period of three months in the winter of 57-58 that Paul, having been made aware of the developing apostasy in Galatia, wrote his epistle to the church there. "One argument advanced in favor of Corinth as the place of writing is the close resemblance in subject matter between this epistle and that to the Romans, which was written during Paul's third visit to Corinth. Justification by faith is the theme of both epistles, and both deal at length with the distinction between 'the law' and the gospel" (*SDA Bible Commentary*, vol. 6, p. 932).

"While tarrying at Corinth, Paul had cause for serious apprehension concerning some of the churches already established. Through the influence of false teachers who had arisen among the believers in Jerusalem, division, heresy, and sensualism were rapidly gaining ground among the believers in Galatia. These false teachers were mingling Jewish traditions with the truths of the gospel. Ignoring the decision of the general council at Jerusalem, they urged upon the Gentile converts the observance of the ceremonial law" (*The Acts of the Apostles*, p. 383).

Paul an Apostle

By implication, Galatians chapter 1 presents a number of ways *not* to be right with God. One way is to reject the authority of the apostles as inspired witnesses to the truth of the gospel. Paul reminded the Galatians that, because he was an apostle, directly appointed by Christ and the Father (see Galatians 1:1), possessing as much inspired authority as the other apostles, his message was not only credible but essential for salvation.

Paul knew that if the Galatians rejected his apostolic authority they would reject his message. Evidently the legalistic Jewish Christians who had opposed the decisions of the Jerusalem Council were trying to convince the Galatians that, because Paul was not a true apostle, his message was a human invention.

"Paul an apostle—not from men nor through man, but through Jesus Christ and God the Father" (Galatians 1:1, RSV). What is an apostle? The Greek word translated *apostle* means "an ambassador, a delegate, a messenger, an envoy, one who is sent." There is a sense in which every Christian is an apostle for Jesus Christ. We are all sent into the world to teach the gospel (see Matthew 28:19, 20). But the term *apostle* is particularly applied to those who have received direct revelations from Jesus Christ.

Paul connected his position as an apostle with the special revelations given him by Christ. "Am I not an apostle? Have I not seen Jesus our Lord?" he asked (1 Corinthians 9:1, RSV). The other apostles had associated with Christ during His earthly ministry. Paul had seen the risen Jesus on the Damascus road (see Acts 9:1-9), and he had received many inspired visions.

Paul reminded the Corinthians of his calling when they were in danger of wandering from the message he had taught them. He wrote to the Corinthians: "I must boast; there is nothing to be gained by it, but I will go on to visions and revelations of the Lord" (2 Corinthians 12:1, RSV). He then referred to a man who, years before, had been given visions of heavenly things. He was that man. "To keep me from being too elated by the abundance of revelations," he adds, "a thorn was given me in the flesh" (2 Corinthians 12:7, RSV). "I was not at all inferior to these superlative apostles, even though I am nothing. The signs of a true apostle were performed among you in all patience, with signs and wonders and mighty works" (2 Corinthians 12:11, 12, RSV). The many direct revelations from Christ had conferred upon Paul apostolic authority. Paul's message was inspired, absolute truth because it came directly from Jesus Christ Himself.

Like the Galatians, we can fail to be right with God because we do not accept the apostolic authority of the men who wrote the New Testament. Many have serious doubts about the absolute truthfulness of the New Testament message of salvation by faith in Jesus Christ, because they question the inspired authority of the apostles.

A few years ago I received a visit from two ministers of the Unification Church. They wanted to tell me what they believed and why. I listened to them for an hour and a half as they asserted that, by making ourselves perfect as was Christ, we can become Christs. There is not only one Christ, they argued; we all may be Christs.

When my turn came to speak, I asked them whether they accepted everything the Bible teaches, and they assured me that they did. Then I presented the Bible evidence that only One is Christ and that we can have victory over sin and have spiritual power only as we accept Him into our hearts by the Holy Spirit. I quoted much from the apostle Paul.

They became quite angry, and asked, "What's so great about the apostle Paul?" When I pointed out that he had written a large share of the New Testament that they had agreed to accept as truth, they became even more agitated. Unfortunately their teachings meant more to them than those of the inspired apostle. Because they had rejected his apostolic authority, they had rejected his message.

The Death and Resurrection of Christ

It is a fact that Christ died for our sins and rose from the dead to be our heavenly Mediator. We fail to be right with God if we reject that. Paul emphasized this central gospel truth at the beginning of his epistle to the Galatians: "Paul an apostle—not from men nor through man, but through Jesus

Christ and God the Father, who raised him from the dead. . . ." "[Our Lord Jesus Christ] . . . gave himself for our sins to deliver us from the present evil age" (Galatians 1:1, 3, 4, RSV).

In effect the Galatians were rejecting the very heart of the gospel. The Judaizers had convinced them that they could not be saved if they did not observe the Jewish ceremonial law. Paul and the other apostles consistently taught that the ceremonial law pointed forward to the death and ministry of Jesus Christ (compare Ephesians 2:14-16; Hebrews 10:1-10). The ceremonial law was temporary because the shadow met its reality in Christ. By rejecting that truth the Galatians were underestimating the great significance of the cross and the ministry of Christ.

We underestimate the significance of the death of Christ when we deny that He bore on the cross the legal punishment for our sins. The message of Scripture is unequivocally clear that Jesus Christ suffered the guilt of our sins (see Isaiah 53:6; 1 Peter 2:24; 1 John 2:2; 4:10; 2 Corinthians 5:21).

Jesus showed us how to live and how to die. His life and death revealed the infinite love of God for all humanity. His life and death are the greatest possible revelations of the character of God (see John 14:8-11). But His life, death, and heavenly ministry mean more than that! Because He bore the legal punishment for all human sin, we can be entirely free from guilt (see Romans 8:1). And we can have His righteous presence living within as our qualification for eternal life (see Romans 8:9, 10).

Salvation by Grace Alone

We can fail to be right with God by rejecting the Bible message of salvation by grace alone. "Grace be to you and peace from God the Father, and from our Lord Jesus Christ," Paul wrote to the Galatians (Galatians 1:3). At this point Paul is touching upon the theme of his epistle. There would have been no need for the epistle if the Galatians had depended upon Christ's grace for salvation instead of upon their own works.

The message of salvation by grace alone, made possible by

Christ's death, resurrection, and heavenly ministry, is at the very heart of the New Testament gospel (see Ephesians 2:8-10; Romans 3:24). We speak of "righteousness by faith," because when we believe in Christ, we receive the saving gift of His righteousness. In fact, our faith is called forth by His grace. We could not believe but for the convincing work of the Holy Spirit in our hearts (see John 16:8). The gift of faith and the gift of Christ's righteousness are gifts of grace; a gift that is thoroughly undeserved, given by the beneficent generosity of an infinitely loving God (see Romans 5:17, 20, 21).

The result is peace with God. "Grace be to you and peace from God the Father, and from our Lord Jesus Christ" (Galatians 1:3). "Being justified by faith, we have peace with God through our Lord Jesus Christ: by whom also we have access by faith into this grace wherein we stand" (Romans 5:1, 2). Grace engenders our faith; we exercise faith by accepting Christ as Saviour and Lord; and His divine presence in our hearts brings peace with God. Restless discontent, festering guilt, and harbored bitterness give place to restful assurance, loving confidence, and conscious innocence.

We can fail to be right with God when we reject Christ's grace as the power in our hearts for victory over sin. Grace is indeed God's unmerited favor; but it is more than that. It is God's power working within us, keeping us in close conformity to His will, and enabling us to work for others. "God is able to make all grace abound toward you; that ye, always having all sufficiency in all things, may abound to every good work" (2 Corinthians 9:8).

Paul spoke of "the exceeding grace of God in you" (2 Corinthians 9:14). He wrote of the spiritual enrichment "in all utterance, and in all knowledge," resulting from the grace of Christ in the heart of the believers (1 Corinthians 1:5). Peter spoke of growth in grace (see 2 Peter 3:18).

You cannot be enriched by something or grow in something unless it is within. Christ's grace is the power of His divine presence imparted to struggling sinners, enabling them to conquer sin and live victoriously for Him.

"The grace of Christ in the soul is developing traits of character that are the opposite of selfishness,—traits that will refine, ennoble, and enrich the life" (*Thoughts From the Mount of Blessing*, p. 82). "The greatest manifestation that men and women can make of the grace and power of Christ is made when the natural man becomes a partaker of the divine nature, and through the power that the grace of Christ imparts, overcomes the corruption that is in the world through lust" (*Counsels to Parents, Teachers, and Students*, pp. 251, 252).

Only One Gospel

We can fail to be right with God when we accept a variation of the one true gospel. Paul expressed his shock that the Galatians had departed from Christ by espousing a false gospel. They had turned to a "different gospel—not that there is another gospel, but there are some who trouble you and want to pervert the gospel of Christ" (Galatians 1:6, 7, RSV). Twice Paul warned the Galatians that God's curse rests upon those who teach any variation of the one true gospel that he had taught them (see Galatians 1:8, 9).

Now, of course, we do not have any right to curse others who reject the true gospel (see Matthew 5:44; Romans 12:14). Only God has the right to pronounce a curse upon those who reject Christ and His truth (see Matthew 25:41; 2 Peter 2:14; Revelation 22:18). The curse pronounced by Paul, the inspired apostle, is Christ's curse. Later in the Galatian epistle, Paul explained that those who are attempting to be saved by their own works are under a curse (see Galatians 3:10). The point is that guilt is abolished only as we accept the sacrifice of Jesus for us. "Christ redeemed us from the curse of the law, having become a curse for us" (Galatians 3:13, RSV). But if we attempt to modify the divine plan by trying to earn forgiveness and salvation by our works, our guilt remains; the curse of the law that we have broken still rests upon us.

Although we do not curse anyone, God would have us distinguish between truth and error. By adherence to the Word of God we are to detect and expose error, warning of God's curse upon those who refuse truth (see Isaiah 8:20; Matthew 7:15-20; 24:24; Titus 1:9-13).

"Those who engage in the work of God's cause today will meet just such trials as Paul endured in his work. By the same boastful and deceptive work Satan will seek to draw converts from the faith. Theories will be brought in that it will not be wise for us to handle. Satan is a cunning worker, and he will bring in subtle fallacies to darken and confuse the mind and root out the doctrines of salvation. Those who do not accept the Word of God just as it reads, will be snared in his trap.

"Today we need to speak the truth with holy boldness. The testimony borne to the early church by the Lord's messenger, His people are to hear in this time: 'Though we, or an angel from heaven, preach any other gospel unto you than that which we have preached unto you, let him be accursed' (Galatians 1:8)" (*Selected Messages*, bk. 2, p. 52).

As evidence that the gospel that he had taught the Galatians was the true one, Paul emphasized that he did not receive it from any human being. "It came through a revelation of Jesus Christ" (Galatians 1:12, RSV). Paul had been lost within legalistic Judaism (see Galatians 1:13, 14). But when Christ called him he responded (see Galatians 1:15, 16). He did not "confer with flesh and blood" (verse 16). He did not sit at the feet of the apostles. He went to Arabia, where Christ revealed to him the gospel he was to preach to the Gentiles (verse 17). "He emptied his soul of the prejudices and traditions that had hitherto shaped his life, and received instruction from the Source of truth. Jesus communed with him and established him in the faith, bestowing upon him a rich measure of wisdom and grace" (*The Acts of the Apostles*, pp. 125, 126).

Three years after his conversion, Paul went to Jerusalem. Although he stayed fifteen days with Peter, he did not receive his gospel from him or from any other apostle (see Galatians 1:18-20; compare Acts 9:26-29). Most of his time in Jerusalem he spent preaching.

While praying in the temple, Paul received a command from Christ to leave Jerusalem (see Acts 22:17, 18). The Jews were planning to kill him (see Acts 9:29). He left for Tarsus, where he spent the next few years (see Acts 9:30; Galatians 1:21-24).

Summary

Galatians chapter 1 is a stern rebuke to the Galatians for deserting the gospel taught by the apostle Paul. Ignoring his apostolic authority, depreciating the significance of Calvary, and practicing salvation by works, they had turned to a false gospel. Paul reminded them that the one true gospel that he had taught them came not from man, but by direct revelation from Jesus Christ.

Chapter 3
Faith and Action

Galatians 2:1-14; Acts 15:1, 2

A Pennsylvania farmer once described how his dogs behaved when they became possessed with sheep-killing fever. Even the best dogs could be afflicted by this problem. At night such a dog would slink out of the farmyard and attack unsuspecting sheep in a nearby field. Before leaving for the night's escapade the guilty dog would run around the farmyard trying to coax other dogs to go with him. During the day he would be especially docile, friendly, and cooperative around the house and the barn. The obvious intention was to convince his master that he could not possibly be the killer.

How human animals can be! The sheep-killing dog illustrates the essence of hypocrisy. The aim is to act in a manner that is satisfying to yourself, even though the behavior is contrary to what others have come to expect of you, without anyone's guessing that there is a conflict between your spiritual commitments and your manner of life. The hypocrite is a kind of split personality. Faith and action have become discordant; professed faith says one thing, but action says quite another.

Sometimes people can be in this condition without even realizing it. They have become so accustomed to giving credence to the Christian faith and so habitually involved in a way of life that contradicts the faith, that they can no longer see the enormity of their inconsistency. Take, for example, the church elder who speaks and prays well in church, but whose moral and ethical conduct does not match his profession. Consider the church member who faithfully returns tithe, attends prayer meeting, and strictly observes the Sabbath, but who takes pleasure in watching bawdy television shows. And what about the minister who preaches eloquently but who forgets to treat his wife as a real person and who is a petty domestic dictator with his children.

Hypocrisy is a spiritual disease. The apostle Paul was confronted by the hypocrisy of the legalistic Jewish Christians who were doing all they could to lead the Galatian believers away from the true gospel. These Judaizers had heard the decisions of the Jerusalem Council. They had been made aware that the apostles endorsed Paul's teachings. But they persistently refused to believe that a Gentile could be saved without observing the ceremonial law, including the ritualistic practice of circumcision. The legalists professed to be genuine Christians who accepted Jesus as Saviour and Lord. Yet they lived in a manner quite contrary to the principles of His teaching. They were church-splitters, accusers of the brethren, self-righteous egotists, who claimed great knowledge and piety but who acted in a manner quite inconsistent with their exalted profession.

"The apostle urged the Galatians to leave the false guides by whom they had been misled, and to return to the faith that had been accompanied by unmistakable evidences of divine approval. The men who had attempted to lead them from their belief in the gospel were hypocrites, unholy in heart and corrupt in life. Their religion was made up of a round of ceremonies, through the performance of which they expected to gain the favor of God. They had no desire for a gospel that called for obedience to the word, 'Except a man be born again, he cannot see the kingdom of God.' John 3:3. They felt that a religion based on such a doctrine, required too great a sacrifice, and they clung to their errors, deceiving themselves and others" (*The Acts of the Apostles*, pp. 386, 387).

Paul's Faith and Action

The legalists were accusing Paul of the very sin of which they were guilty. "He claims to be a true Christian," they argued, "but he teaches a man-made, innovative gospel quite different from that accepted by Christ's apostles." In other words, they accused Paul of hypocrisy and deception.

Paul's answer in his letter to the Galatians was that he had received his message directly from Christ (see Galatians 1:16) and that the apostles at the Jerusalem Council had endorsed his teaching as thoroughly consistent with their own (see Galatians 2:1-10). Paul was no hypocrite! His faith and action were in complete agreement. Because he taught salvation by grace alone, he refused to induct the Gentile converts into the observance of the ceremonial law. Because he believed in the primacy of faith and grace as the means of salvation, he refused to teach or practice a system of works-righteousness.

Paul pointed out to the Galatians that the only significant visit he had made to the Jerusalem apostles after his conversion was his visit with Barnabas to the Jerusalem Council, fourteen years later (see Galatians 2:1). He had not received his teachings from the apostles during that fourteen-year period. During his first visit to Peter three years after the Damascus road experience, there had been so many other distractions that no one could claim that he had received his teachings then (see Galatians 1:18, 19).

There was a second visit, not mentioned in Galatians, during which Paul and Barnabas took famine relief to the believers in Jerusalem (see Acts 11:28-30). The purpose of this visit was not to discuss the doctrinal problems developing in the church of Antioch. In fact, we are given no indication that the Judaizers had begun their campaign there this early, before Paul's first missionary journey.

By the time the Jerusalem Council began, Paul had been teaching salvation by grace alone for the best part of fourteen years (see Galatians 2:1). And what he taught, he practiced.

Paul at the Jerusalem Council

There can be no serious doubt that Paul's visit to the apostles in Jerusalem, described in Galatians 2:1-10, was his visit to the Jerusalem Council, described in Acts 15. The problem discussed in the two chapters is identical: the division in the church of Antioch caused by the demand of legalists that Gentile converts be circumcised and required to observe the ceremonial law. The occasion and outcome described in the two chapters are the same.

"Paul . . . describes the visit which he made to Jerusalem to secure a settlement of the very questions which are now agitating the churches of Galatia, as to whether the Gentiles should submit to circumcision and keep the ceremonial law. This was the only instance in which he had deferred to the judgment of the other apostles as superior to his own. He had first sought a private interview, in which he set the matter in all its bearings before the leading apostles, Peter, James, and John. With far-seeing wisdom, he concluded that if these men could be led to take a right position, everything would be gained. Had he first presented the question before the whole council, there would have been a division of sentiment. The strong prejudice already excited because he had not enforced circumcision on the Gentiles, would have led many to take a stand against him. Thus the object of his visit would have been defeated, and his usefulness greatly hindered. But the three leading apostles, against whom no such prejudice existed, having themselves been won to the true position, brought the matter before the council, and won from all a concurrence in the decision to leave the Gentiles free from the obligations of the ceremonial law" (*SDA Bible Commentary*, vol. 6, p. 1108).

The date of A.D. 49 for the Jerusalem Council is tentative, as are the other dates for the life of Paul. "Then fourteen years after" may mean fourteen years after his first visit to Jerusalem. This first visit was three years after his conversion (see Galatians 1:18) about A.D. 38. If this is correct, the date for the Jerusalem Council would be A.D. 38 plus fourteen years, or A.D. 52. The reason that we tentatively date the Jerusalem Council fourteen years after Paul's conversion is that Paul's point in Galatians 1 and 2 seems to be that he had no contact with the apostles in general at Jerusalem until fourteen years after his conversion.

Since Paul's message was given by divine revelation, why did the Lord instruct him to submit it to the scrutiny of the church council in Jerusalem (see Galatians 2:2)? Paul went up to Jerusalem "by revelation." That means that in a special revelation to Paul the Lord told him to go. Luke's account of the same incident indicates that "Paul and Barnabas and some of the others *were appointed* to go up to Jerusalem" by the Antioch church (Acts 15:2, RSV, italics supplied). The light that the Lord gives to one person He also gives to His church by the teaching ministry of the Holy Spirit.

"Notwithstanding the fact that Paul was personally taught by God, he had no strained ideas of individual responsibility. While looking to God for direct guidance, he was ever ready to recognize the authority vested in the body of believers united in church fellowship. He felt the need of counsel, and when matters of importance arose, he was glad to lay these before the church and to unite with his brethren in seeking God for wisdom to make right decisions. Even 'the spirits of the prophets,' he declared, 'are subject to the prophets. For God is not the author of confusion, but of peace, as in all churches of the saints,' 1 Corinthians 14:32, 33. With Peter, he taught that all united in church capacity should be 'subject one to another' " (*The Acts of the Apostles*, p. 200).

What unity there would be if the church today were willing to follow this principle! Individuals would hesitate to conclude that they have new light that the church at large does not have. They would less likely insist that the church could be put back on track if the leaders and members would only accept this special truth. The message from Paul's attitude and experience underlines the truth that the Lord is leading a people, not just one person here or there. Our confidence in Christ's leading and teaching ministry should call forth distrust of our personal judgments and awaken confidence in the decisions of the church body as a whole.

"God has made His church on the earth a channel of light, and through it He communicates His purposes and His will. He does not give to one of His servants an experience independent of and contrary to the experience of the church itself.

Neither does He give one man a knowledge of His will for the entire church while the church—Christ's body—is left in darkness. In His providence He places His servants in close connection with His church in order that they may have less confidence in themselves and greater confidence in others whom He is leading out to advance His work.

"There have ever been in the church those who are constantly inclined toward individual independence. They seem unable to realize that independence of spirit is liable to lead the human agent to have too much confidence in himself and to trust in his own judgment rather than to respect the counsel and highly esteem the judgment of his brethren, especially of those in the offices that God has appointed for the leadership of His people. God has invested His church with special authority and power, which no one can be justified in disregarding and despising; for he who does this despises the voice of God. . . .

"Every agency will be subordinate to the Holy Spirit, and all the believers will be united in an organized and well-directed effort to give to the world the glad tidings of the grace of God" (*The Acts of the Apostles*, pp. 163, 164).

Note Paul's attitude to the "false brethren" who were attempting to persuade the Jerusalem Council members that his message was erroneous and that the Gentiles should be expected to observe the ceremonial law (see Galatians 2:4, 5). He knew that the gospel committed to him was absolute truth, and he "did not yield submission even for a moment" (Galatians 2:5, RSV) to these legalistic brethren. Opposition to those who are rejecting revealed truth should be Christ-like but unyielding. The Christian church is not built upon compromise with error (see *The Acts of the Apostles*, p. 386).

Paul's words recorded in Galatians 2:6 have aroused concern as to his real attitude to his fellow apostles. "From those who were reputed to be something (what they were makes no difference to me; God shows no partiality)—those, I say, who were of repute added nothing to me" (Galatians 2:6, RSV). As we have seen, Paul did not act independently of his brethren and sisters in the church. His point in Galatians 2:6 is that the leading apostles to whom he presented his case were not the source of his gospel. It came directly from Christ Himself. "The strength of his argument is that, although Paul had not conferred with, or been instructed by, the Twelve, his gospel was nevertheless the same as theirs" (*SDA Bible Commentary*, vol. 6, pp. 945, 946).

The decision of the council was that Paul and Barnabas continue proclaiming salvation by grace alone to the Gentiles. No one was to be required to observe the ceremonial law. The One to whom those ceremonies had pointed had paid the penalty for sin on the cross and was now ministering in the heavenly sanctuary. Although the Gentile convert Titus had accompanied Paul to the council, the leading apostles saw no need for him to be circumcised (see Galatians 2:3). Faith was demonstrated in action. They practiced what they preached and urged Paul and Barnabas to do the same (compare Galatians 2:7-10; Acts 15:19-29).

Peter's Action Contradicted Faith

When Paul, Barnabas, and Titus went back to Antioch, Peter paid them a visit. Trouble arose when Peter, who had been eating and associating freely with Gentiles, turned away from them because the legalists had arrived from Jerusalem. If Jewish ceremonial observances were no longer necessary, why should Peter capitulate to prejudices that separated him from Gentile converts? Imagine the reaction in the mostly Gentile church of Antioch to Peter's action. They would feel that he had virtually nullified the decisions of the Jerusalem Council. They would feel like second-class Christians, inferior to Jewish Christians and only barely tolerated by a leading apostle.

Paul's rebuke was in order, and Peter responded positively to it. "Peter saw the error into which he had fallen, and immediately set about repairing the evil that had been wrought, so far as was in his power. God, who knows the end from the beginning, permitted Peter to reveal this weakness of character in order that the tried apostle might see that there was nothing in himself whereof he might boast" (*The Acts of the Apostles*, p. 198).

Summary

Faith that is not manifested in action is worthless. The Judaizers professed faith in Christ but denied it by their behavior. Paul and the Jerusalem apostles demonstrated their faith in Christ's grace by appropriate action. Peter denied his faith by refusing to eat with Gentiles. When our faith and action are in complete accord, we are Christians in the true sense. Discord between faith and action results in hypocrisy.

Chapter 4
How to Become Right and Stay Right With God

Galatians 2:15-21

As a college teacher, over a period of years I had many students in my classes who had recently given their lives to Christ. They had come out of many different backgrounds. Some had been involved in the drug scene, living to satisfy their physical desires, unaware that the Lord has a wonderful plan for them. Rock music, communal living, and the immediate demand for sensual satisfaction were the imperatives in their way of life. When Christ was able to break through to their hearts, the whole scene changed. They came to hate their old habits and to love the purity and tenderness of Jesus. They were right with God. When I knew them, they were demonstrating a profound dedication to the principles of the Sermon on the Mount.

Often I would ask these particular students, "What is it about Christianity that is most important to you?" The answer invariably would be something like this: "I now have a power that I did not have before. When I was outside of Christ, I was a victim of my impulses, unable to think straight and unable to break free from the habits and hungers that controlled me. The most impressive thing about Christianity to me is the presence of Christ with me. He gives me the power to live a new life of fulfillment and use-fulness."

There are certain basic questions to which these young people had found the answers: (1) What does Christ expect of me? (2) How can I fulfill Christ's expectations? (3) What does forgiveness do for me? (4) What is the "new birth"? (5) Can I be holy now? (6) How can I grow in holiness? (7) What if I fall? (8) How can I have Christ with me always?

These questions relate to the part of Paul's epistle to the Galatians that we will discuss in this chapter (see Galatians 2:15-21).

What Does Christ Expect of Me?

Christ expects me to be righteous. The Bible teaches that only righteous people will have a part in the kingdom of heaven. Jesus said that the wicked will be destroyed forever, but the "righteous" will go "into life eternal" (Matthew 25:46). "There shall in no wise enter into it any thing that defileth, neither whatsoever worketh abomination, or maketh a lie: but they which are written in the Lamb's book of life" (Revelation 21:27). Sin is alien to heaven. People who cherish sin would be very unhappy in heaven. A man traveling in a foreign country and unable to buy the kind of food he enjoys is usually quite unhappy. He is glad when the time comes to return home. Likewise a person who loves sin would never adjust to the sin-less environment of heaven.

The book of Hebrews speaks of "holiness, without which no man shall see the Lord" (12:14). Holiness is righteousness. It is purity of heart and conduct. In the Sermon on the Mount Jesus said that our righteousness must exceed that of the scribes and Pharisees (see Matthew 5:20). Then He illustrated what He meant. It is not enough to refrain from killing; we must not harbor hate or bitterness in our hearts (see Matthew 5:21, 22). It is not enough to refrain from overt acts of im-morality. Lustfully looking upon the opposite sex is sin (see Matthew 5:28). So righteousness, as Jesus defined it, is a pure attitude of mind that manifests itself in outward acts accept-able to God. Righteousness is the opposite of sin. Paul wrote,

"Awake to righteousness, and sin not; for some have not the knowledge of God" (1 Corinthians 15:34). Since sin is the transgression of God's law (see 1 John 3:4), righteousness involves obedience to His law. Paul taught that Christ died, "that the righteousness of the law might be fulfilled in us" (Romans 8:4).

Peter exclaims, "If the righteous scarcely be saved, where shall the ungodly and the sinner appear?" (1 Peter 4:18). The Greek of the passage means, "If a righteous person is saved *with difficulty*," how will it fare for the ungodly person? The qualification for salvation is righteousness. But how in this world, in which sin of one shade or another is so prevalent, can a person ever reach that standard?

How Can I Fulfill Christ's Expectations?

The question is, How can I be righteous so that I will be qualified for eternal life? The Jewish legalists who were opposing Paul's teaching in Galatia argued that a person becomes righteous simply by his efforts to keep the law. They argued that, if sin is breaking God's law, surely righteousness is obedience to God's law. Therefore, we become righteous as we make the effort to obey God's law.

In his letter to the Galatians, Paul flatly contradicted that idea. "We ourselves, who are Jews by birth and not Gentile sinners, yet who know that a man is not justified by works of the law but through faith in Jesus Christ, even we have believed in Christ Jesus, in order to be justified by faith in Christ, and not by works of the law, because by works of the law shall no one be justified" (Galatians 2:15, 16, RSV).

Law keeping is not the means of righteousness, for two reasons: (1) All of us have broken God's law in the past, so present and future obedience cannot atone for past sin; (2) none of us has the ability to obey God's law perfectly apart from the power of Christ. Jesus taught that very clearly: "Apart from me you can do nothing" (John 15:5, RSV). We can overcome sin only through the empowering presence of Christ in our hearts.

Justification answers that twofold problem. When Christ

justifies a sinner, the guilt of past sins is taken away. Because Jesus died "for our sins: and not for ours only, but also for the sins of the whole world" (1 John 2:2), we are entirely forgiven when we accept Him as Saviour and Lord. But justification involves more than the abolition of our guilt. It also involves the transformation of our hearts. In justification a believer is given purity of life and the power to obey Christ's law.

When Paul said that we are "justified by faith in Christ, *and not by works of the law*" (Galatians 2:16, RSV, italics supplied), he did not intend us to conclude that, therefore, the law of God was abolished at the cross. Held by some Christians today, this unbiblical teaching is the very opposite of that taught by the Galatian legalists. Today the antinomians (anti-law exponents) would have us believe that the Ten Commandments were done away with at the cross. That teaching is contradicted all through Paul's writings, and the writings of the other apostles. Paul taught that, since the cross, the law continues to point out our sin, because it is still God's standard of righteousness (see Romans 7:7, 12, 14).

Faith in Christ does not destroy God's law; it results in its being established in our hearts. "Do we then overthrow the law by this faith? By no means! On the contrary, we uphold the law" (Romans 3:31, RSV). Christ died "in order that the just requirement of the law might be fulfilled in us, who walk not according to the flesh but according to the Spirit" (Romans 8:4, RSV).

The word *justified*, used three times in Galatians 2:16 does not mean much to twentieth-century readers. It is possible to read all kinds of meanings into the word. The important issue is to discover how Paul defines the word.

The Greek word translated "justified" in Galatians 2:16 comes from the Greek verb (*dikaioo*) that corresponds to the noun *righteousness* (*dikaiosune*) and the adjective *righteous* (*dikaios*). We can illustrate the relationship between these words by noting the relationship between the English words, *to beautify* (verb), *beauty* (noun), and *beautiful* (adjective). When you *beautify* your garden you give it *beauty*, so that now it is *beautiful*. In the same way, when God *justifies* us, He gives His *righteousness*, so that we are *righteous*. This is what it means to have present salvation in Christ. God does not bestow righteousness upon us *as a reward* for our efforts to keep His law. He bestows righteousness upon us *as the power* to keep His law.

What Does Forgiveness Do for Me?

When a person is "justified" (see Galatians 2:16) his sins are forgiven. Justification and forgiveness are one and the same experience. Preaching at Antioch in Pisidia on his first missionary journey, Paul identified forgiveness and justification. Acts 13:38, 39 may be translated from Greek text: "Let it be known to you, men, brethren, that through this man forgiveness (pardon, release from captivity) of sins is being proclaimed to you; from everything from which you were not able to be justified by the law of Moses, by this man those who believe are justified." Christ justifies us by forgiving our sins.

In his epistle to the Romans, Paul emphasized the same truth. Justification is God's act of reckoning righteousness to the penitent sinner. This is forgiveness: "So also David pronounces a blessing upon the man to whom God reckons righteousness apart from works: 'Blessed are those whose iniquities are forgiven, and whose sins are covered; blessed is the man against whom the Lord will not reckon his sin'" (Romans 4:6, 7, RSV).

"Pardon and justification are one and the same thing. Through faith, the believer passes from the position of a rebel, a child of sin and Satan, to the position of a loyal subject of Christ Jesus, not because of an inherent goodness, but because Christ receives him as His child by adoption. The sinner receives the forgiveness of his sins, because these sins are borne by his Substitute and Surety. . . . The grace of Christ is freely to justify the sinner without merit or claim on his part. Justification is a full, complete pardon of sin. The moment a sinner accepts Christ by faith, that moment he is pardoned. The righteousness of Christ is imputed to him, and he is no more to doubt God's forgiving grace" (*SDA Bible Commentary*, vol. 6, pp. 1070, 1071).

When another human being forgives us for something we may have said or done, they agree to overlook the past, but they cannot change our hearts. When God forgives us, He not only abolishes our guilt, He also transforms us. Forgiveness in Scripture is both a legal declaration of acquittal and transformation of heart. The Greek word for forgiveness, *aphesis*, means both "pardon, cancellation of an obligation, a punishment, or guilt," and also "release from captivity" (William F. Arndt and F. Wilbur Gingrich, *A Greek-English Lexicon of the New Testament*, p. 124).

Jesus' work was to release Satan's captives by forgiving their sins. Luke 4:18 records that in the synagogue in Nazareth one Sabbath day Jesus read Isaiah 61:1, 2: " 'The Spirit of the Lord is upon me, because he has anointed me to preach good news to the poor. He has sent me to proclaim *release* [forgiveness] to the captives and recovering of sight to the blind, *to set at liberty those who are oppressed* [to send forth the oppressed in forgiveness]' " (Luke 4:18, RSV, italics supplied). Twice in Luke's version of the passage the Greek word for "forgiveness" is used. It is translated in the English Bible by "release" because the Greek word means both "forgiveness" and "release from captivity." Jesus' forgiveness released sinners from Satan's dominion.

Paul taught that deliverance "from the dominion of darkness," or redemption, is "the forgiveness of sins" (Colossians 1:13, 14, RSV). The kind of forgiveness that David sought after his sin of adultery involved not only relief from guilt but also transformation of heart (see Psalms 51:2, 7, 10).

"God's forgiveness is not merely a judicial act by which He sets us free from condemnation. It is not only forgiveness *for* sin, but reclaiming *from* sin. *It is the outflow of redeeming love that transforms the heart.* David had the true conception of forgiveness when he prayed, 'Create in me a clean heart, O God; and renew a right spirit within me.' Psalm 51:10" (*Thoughts From the Mount of Blessing*, p. 114, last italics supplied).

"*To be pardoned in the way that Christ pardons, is not only to be forgiven, but to be renewed in the spirit of our mind.* The

Lord says, 'A new heart will I give unto thee.' The image of Christ is to be stamped upon the very mind, heart, and soul. The apostle says, 'And we have the mind of Christ.' Without the transforming process which can come alone through divine power, the original propensities to sin are left in the heart in all their strength, to forge new chains, to impose a slavery that can never be broken by human power. But men can never enter heaven with their old tastes, inclinations, idols, ideas, and theories" (Ellen G. White, *Review and Herald*, August 19, 1890, italics supplied).

Because forgiveness and justification are one and the same thing, we conclude that justification includes (1) a legal declaration of acquittal in which Christ's righteousness is placed to the penitent sinner's account, and (2) transformation of heart.

What Is the New Birth?

Paul taught that justification includes the new-birth experience. The new birth is not a separate experience that occurs at the same time as justification. The new birth is justification.

Titus 3:5-7 may be translated literally from the Greek text: "Not by works in righteousness which we did, but according to His mercy He *saved* us, by the washing of *rebirth* and renewing of the Holy Spirit, which He poured out upon us richly through Jesus Christ our Saviour, so that, *having been justified* by His grace, we might be heirs according to the hope of eternal life."

How did Christ save us? By transforming us in the new-birth experience, in which the Holy Spirit was poured out upon us. This saving act was His justifying act. "He saved us . . . so that, having been justified by His grace, we might be heirs." His justification was not the result of His saving; it was the same thing as His saving. The result was that we became heirs. How did He save us? "By the washing of rebirth and renewing of the Holy Spirit." How did He justify us? In the same manner, by giving us the new-birth experience. Justification and the new birth are one and the same experience.

As He explained to Nicodemus how to be saved, Jesus used

a figure of speech. Salvation is like being born all over again (see John 3:3-8). Paul used a different figure of speech to illustrate the same truth. As a judge declares a defendant acquitted, so Christ declares us acquitted. But there are differences. Christ declares us innocent, not because we *are* innocent. He places His innocence (righteousness) to our account. But more than that, unlike an earthly judge, when Christ acquits us, He transforms our hearts. We become new creatures because the Holy Spirit has changed our minds. By the divine miracle of His indwelling He has brought us into agreement with the principles of His holy law (see Romans 8:1-4).

"As the sinner, drawn by the power of Christ, approaches the uplifted cross, and prostrates himself before it, there is a new creation. A new heart is given him. He becomes a new creature in Christ Jesus. Holiness finds that it has nothing more to require. God Himself is 'the justifier of him which believeth in Jesus.' Romans 3:26" (*Christ's Object Lessons*, p. 163).

Can I Be Holy Now?

When Christ justifies us, the Holy Spirit comes into our hearts in the new-birth experience. The presence of the Holy Spirit is the presence of Christ and the presence of righteousness in our hearts (see Romans 8:9, 10). Righteousness, the qualification for heaven, is not an intangible quality that is poured upon us. Righteousness is Christ by the Holy Spirit inhabiting the believer's life.

"Righteousness is holiness, likeness to God, and 'God is love.' 1 John 4:16. It is conformity to the law of God, for 'all Thy commandments are righteousness' (Psalm 119:172). . . . The righteousness of God is embodied in Christ. We receive righteousness by receiving Him" (*Thoughts From the Mount of Blessing*, p. 18).

Since righteousness is holiness, and we receive righteousness when we receive Christ, we receive holiness when we receive Christ. We receive Christ and His righteousness when we are justified. Therefore, we receive holiness when we are justified. The Greek word for "holiness" also means "sanctification." Sanctification is often thought of as growth in holiness. And so it is! But it is also the experience of holiness enjoyed by the believer now. There are many more passages in the New Testament that use the verb *to sanctify* in the sense of present holiness in Christ than there are passages that use it in reference to spiritual growth. This is not to depreciate the great importance of spiritual growth. Nevertheless, it is vital to accept the Bible truth that the divinely indwelt Christian has present holiness (sanctification) in Christ.

The thief on the cross was both justified and sanctified. As we have seen, Jesus will take no unholy person to heaven. But He promised the dying thief that he would be in heaven with Him.

Many times in the New Testament sanctification is spoken of as an experience already given to the believer. The Greek text literally translated emphasizes the point. Acts 26:18 speaks of those "who have been sanctified." Paul wrote of the Gentiles having "been sanctified by the Holy Spirit" (Romans 15:16). He wrote of the Corinthians as "having been sanctified in Christ Jesus, called to be saints [or holy ones]" (1 Corinthians 1:2). Yet these very church members were divided by their controversies and prejudices. The point is that they were spoiling the beautiful gift of holiness that had been bestowed upon them by the Holy Spirit. Paul writes of the experience of cleansing that had come to them *in the past*: "You were washed, *you were sanctified*, you were justified in the name of the Lord Jesus Christ and in the Spirit of our God" (1 Corinthians 6:11, RSV, italics supplied). Colossians 2:10 reads, "You are complete [perfect] in Him." Hebrews 10:10, NKJV, says, "We have been sanctified" (compare 1 Thessalonians 2:13; 1 Peter 1:1, 2).

Justification is Christ bestowed; sanctification is Christ possessed. Justification is Christ's gift of Himself to us every day. Sanctification (holiness) is Christ possessed in our hearts every day. Sanctification is the state of present holiness or righteousness in Christ enjoyed by the justified believer.

"True sanctification is harmony with God, oneness with Him in character" (*Testimonies*, vol. 6, p. 350).

"Sanctification is a state of holiness, without and within, being holy and without reserve the Lord's, not in form, but in truth" (*Our High Calling*, p. 214).

How Can I Grow in Holiness?

Scripture also speaks of sanctification as growth in holiness in Christ (see 1 Thessalonians 3:12, 13; 4:1-4; 2 Corinthians 3:18; 2 Peter 3:18). The believer is still a fallen human being (see 1 Corinthians 9:27; Galatians 5:15-17). Sanctification as growth involves constant surrender to Christ so that the Holy Spirit wins the inner war (see *Testimonies*, vol. 4, p. 299).

"We need constantly a fresh revelation of Christ, a daily experience that harmonizes with His teachings. High and holy attainments are within our reach. Continual progress in knowledge and virtue is God's purpose for us. His law is the echo of His own voice, giving to all the invitation, 'Come up higher. Be holy, holier still.' Every day we may advance in perfection of Christian character" (*The Ministry of Healing*, p. 503).

What if I Fall?

Paul considers this question briefly in Galatians 2:17. "If, in our endeavor to be justified in Christ, we ourselves were found to be sinners, is Christ then an agent of sin? Certainly not!" (RSV). Christ has made all the necessary provision to keep us from falling. He "is able to keep you from falling" (Jude 24, RSV). He has given us His Holy Spirit to dwell in our hearts continually. There is no greater power in the universe to enable us to be overcomers. If we fall after receiving justification, is Christ in some way responsible? Paul answers with an emphatic negative.

Then am I lost when I fall into sin? Or do I retain justification like some kind of unbrella over me, despite my occasional dips into the sea of iniquity?

A young man who was leaving for college was given $1,000 by his father to cover his day-by-day expenses. Instead of

using the money wisely, the young man wasted it on unneces-
sary trips in his car and on useless entertainment. He lost his
$1,000, and his father was disappointed in him. But his father
did not stop loving and caring for him. When the boy showed
genuine repentance and willingness to change his spending
habits, the father gave him some more money to help him
through the academic year.

Christ has given us the infinite wealth of His righteousness
by the Holy Spirit. If we choose to sin, we lose His presence in
our hearts, and we lose justification. Christ is not "an agent
[servant] of sin" (Galatians 2:17). He does not justify us so
that we can have the license to commit sin occasionally
without being separated from His righteousness. But when we
sin, He does not disown us and stop caring for us.

"God requires that we confess our sins, and humble our
hearts before Him; but at the same time we should have confidence in Him as a tender Father, who will not forsake those
who put their trust in Him. . . .

"God does not give us up because of our sins. We may make
mistakes, and grieve His Spirit; but when we repent, and
come to Him with contrite hearts, He will not turn us away.
There are hindrances to be removed. Wrong feelings have
been cherished, and there have been pride, self-sufficiency,
impatience, and murmurings. All these separate us from God.
Sins must be confessed; there must be a deeper work of grace
in the heart. Those who feel weak and discouraged may become strong men of God, and do noble work for the Master.
But they must work from a high standpoint; they must be in-
fluenced by no selfish motives" (*Selected Messages*, bk. 1,
pp. 350, 351).

Paul wrote that when you are under grace, "sin will have no
dominion over you" (Romans 6:14, RSV). Obviously, if we commit sin, it does have dominion over us, and we are not under
grace.

"While God can be just, and yet justify the sinner through
the merits of Christ, no man can cover his soul with the garments of Christ's righteousness while practicing known sins,
or neglecting known duties. God requires the entire surrender

of the heart, before justification can take place; and in order for man to retain justification, there must be continual obedience, through active, living faith that works by love and purifies the soul" (*Selected Messages*, bk. 1, p. 366).

"If I build up again those things which I tore down, then I prove myself a transgressor" (Galatians 2:18). What did Paul destroy that he did not want to build up again? The life of attempted righteousness by works was destroyed for Paul once he found Christ. If he were now to capitulate to the demands of the Judaizers, he would lose the empowering presence of Christ in his heart as the source of victory over sin. He would become a transgressor all over again. Self-righteousness is no righteousness, and no righteousness is sin.

How Can I Have Christ With Me Always?

When we are justified, we die to the law in the sense that we are no longer under its condemnation, nor are we misusing it as the means of righteousness and salvation (see Galatians 2:19). As was pointed out earlier, the law remains as God's standard of righteousness, which is now attainable through the power of the indwelling Christ.

As Christ was crucified, so are we when we receive justification. "I have been crucified with Christ" (Galatians 2:20, RSV). Paul wrote to the Romans: "He who died, has been justified from sin" (Romans 6:7, literal translation). The death of the "old man" of sin is justification. As our sin took the life of Jesus, so His righteousness, as it is brought into our hearts by the Holy Spirit, puts to death our old life of sinning.

"It is no longer I who live, but Christ who lives in me; and the life I now live in the flesh I live by faith in the Son of God, who loved me and gave himself for me" (Galatians 2:20, RSV). Christ came to live in me when I was justified. He continues to live in me as I live daily by faith in Him. "Though our outer nature [physical self] is wasting away, our inner nature [spiritual self] is being renewed every day" (2 Corinthians 4:16, RSV).

"Now that you have given yourself to Jesus, do not draw back, do not take yourself away from Him, but day by day say,

'I am Christ's; I have given myself to Him;' and ask Him to give you His Spirit and keep you by His grace. As it is by giving yourself to God, and believing Him, that you become His child, so you are to live in Him. The apostle says, 'As ye have therefore received Christ Jesus the Lord, so walk ye in Him.' Colossians 2:6" (*Steps to Christ*, p. 52).

If after being saved by Christ's grace, you try to live by your own works, you are bound to lose His presence in your heart. Salvation by faith (grace) must be followed by a life of faith (grace). The message is one of total dependence upon Christ for grace to live for Him in every situation of life. "I do not frustrate the grace of God: for if righteousness come by the law, then Christ is dead in vain" (Galatians 2:21).

How do we live by faith? By turning to Jesus daily, hourly, moment by moment. We commune with Him as we work and as we relax. Daily we receive messages from His Word as wisdom for the challenges of life. Christ is to be our closest companion, our ever-present friend.

Summary

Justification includes two elements: (1) Legal acquittal for the guilt of our past sins; (2) the new-birth experience in which we are transformed by the Holy Spirit. Justfication causes sanctification. In justification, Christ's righteousness is bestowed upon us by the Holy Spirit. Because righteousness is holiness, when we receive Christ in justification, we receive present holiness or sanctification. Then we live and grow in the same manner in which we have begun—not by our own unaided efforts, but by faith in Christ, who lives continually in our hearts.

Chapter 5
How God Imputes Righteousness

Galatians 3:1-9

When my wife and I came from Australia to the United States in 1962 with our two little boys, we were not sure that we could survive financially. We had budgeted for one year, but had very limited funds to meet everyday expenses. Fortunately my employer had generously agreed to deposit $2,200 in my account at Andrews University. When we arrived on campus I went to the business office and joyfully discovered that the money was available. The clerk there wrote me a check sufficient to meet our immediate expenses: food, rent, school fees, and seminary fees for me. A little money had to go a long way, but we would have been in dire straits without it.

Money placed in my account represented a legal contract. Because the money was deposited in my name, it was legally mine. But the fact that the books in the business office recorded that a certain amount had been credited to me did me no good at all until I drew the money out and used it to supply the needs of my family. The money credited to me represented spending power.

This illustrates what the Bible means when it says that Christ imputes His righteousness to us. Because all our personal righteousness is unrighteousness (see Isaiah 64:6) and totally unacceptable to God, Christ's perfect righteousness is placed to our account when, by faith, we accept Him as

Saviour and Lord. But the crediting of His righteousness to our account in heaven would not save us if we remained in our sins. When Christ credits His righteousness to us He gives us power to live for Him. He bestows Himself upon us so that not only do we have the assurance that past debts are taken care of, but also, through Him, we have the means in our power not to incur debts in the future. Credited or imputed righteousness represents spiritual power bestowed upon the believer so that his life is made and may remain right with God.

This is the burden of Paul's message in the passage we are considering in this chapter (see Galatians 3:1-9).

Justification Depends on the Crucifixion

"O foolish Galatians!" Paul begins, "who has bewitched you, before whose eyes Jesus Christ was publicly portrayed as crucified?" (Galatians 3:1, RSV). Paul was amazed that the Galatians could so soon turn away from the experience made possible by the cross. When Jesus died for us, He bore the punishment for our sins (see 1 Peter 2:24; Isaiah 53:6; 2 Corinthians 5:21). When the guilt of the world was placed upon Him, the resulting separation from His Father involved infinitely intense agony. Even if the world should go on for another thousand years (perish the thought!) Christ's death was sufficient to atone for all human sin. "He is the expiation [the One who paid the price] for our sins, and not for ours only but also for the sins of the whole world" (1 John 2:2, RSV).

Why try to earn forgiveness when it is given as a free gift to those who accept Jesus? The penalty has been paid, salvation has been earned by Christ. Why try to undo the effectiveness of His saving work by attempting to use law keeping as your means of salvation? Paul rightly regarded legalism as irrational. No wonder he spoke so frankly to the Galatians!

"When God pardons the sinner, remits the punishment he deserves, and treats him as though he had not sinned, He receives him into divine favor, and justifies him through the merits of Christ's righteousness. *The sinner can be justified only through faith in the atonement made through God's dear Son, who became a sacrifice for the sins of the guilty world.* No

one can be justified by any works of his own. He can be
delivered from the guilt of sin, from the condemnation of the
law, from the penalty of transgression, only by virtue of the
suffering, death, and resurrection of Christ. Faith is the only
condition upon which justification can be obtained, and faith
includes not only belief but trust" (*Selected Messages*, bk. 1,
p. 389, italics supplied).

The cross is effective for us only as we are willing to receive
the blessings that result from it. We were not saved at the cross
two thousand years ago. The cross makes possible our salvation
from sin today when we accept Jesus' sacrifice, confess our sins,
and receive Him into our hearts by the Holy Spirit. "*Those who
receive* the abundance of grace and the free gift of righteousness
reign in life through the one man Jesus Christ" (Romans 5:17,
RSV, italics supplied). "*If we confess our sins*, he is faithful and
just to forgive us our sins, and to cleanse us from all
unrighteousness" (1 John 1:9, italics supplied).

"It is not enough to believe *about* Him; you must believe *in*
Him. You must rely wholly upon His saving grace" (*Testimonies*, vol. 5, p. 49).

"When we speak of faith, there is a distinction that should
be borne in mind. There is a kind of belief that is wholly distinct from faith. The existence and power of God, the truth of
His word, are facts that even Satan and his hosts cannot at
heart deny. The Bible says that 'the devils also believe, and
tremble;' but this is not faith. James 2:19. Where there is not
only a belief in God's word, but a submission of the will to
Him; where the heart is yielded to Him, the affections fixed
upon Him, there is faith—faith that works by love and purifies
the soul. Through this faith the heart is renewed in the image
of God" (*Steps to Christ*, p. 63).

The Work of the Holy Spirit in Justification

Paul introduces the Holy Spirit as the agent in justification:
"Let me ask you only this: Did you receive the Spirit by works
of the law, or by hearing with faith? Are you so foolish?
Having begun with the Spirit, are you now ending with the
flesh?" (Galatians 3:2, 3, RSV).

Notice the context of this statement:

Galatians 2:16: We are justified by faith in Christ, not by works of law.

Galatians 2:19: Justification by faith is death to sin and resurrection to a new life in God.

Galatians 2:20: Justification is allowing Christ to crucify our "old man of sin" and permitting Him to come into our lives.

Galatians 2:21: Justification is the means by which we become righteous.

Galatians 3:1: Justification is made possible by Calvary.

Galatians 3:2, 3: Justification by faith is reception of the Holy Spirit.

We begin with the Spirit, as the Galatians did, when we believe in Christ and receive the new-birth experience. The transforming work of the Holy Spirit is justification. Paul's discussion in Galatians 2 and 3 agrees completely with the definition of justification he provides in Titus 3:5-7: We were saved ("justified," verse 7) "through the washing of *rebirth* and renewal by the Holy Spirit, whom he poured out on us generously through Jesus Christ our Savior" (NIV).

The same truth is clearly taught in the book of Romans. "Any one who does not have the Spirit of Christ does not belong to him" (Romans 8:9, RSV). Does the unjustified person belong to Christ? Indeed, no! Does the justified person belong to Christ? Of course! The justified person is the one who has allowed the Holy Spirit to come and dwell within his life. "You are not in the flesh [unjustified], you are in the Spirit [justified], if in fact the Spirit of God dwells in you. . . . But if Christ is in you, although your bodies are dead because of sin, your spirits are alive because of righteousness" (Romans 8:9, 10, RSV). Justification is reception of Christ's righteousness.

How is that accomplished? When the Spirit dwells in our hearts, Christ is in our hearts, and His divine presence is righteousness in our hearts. Paul exclaimed with joy: Christ "is made unto us wisdom, and righteousness [justification], and sanctification, and redemption" (1 Corinthians 1:30).

Paul defines righteousness by faith in Romans 10:6-10. It is the writing of the law of God on the heart of the believer (verses 6-8). It is salvation (verse 9). The Greek of the next verse translates literally: "With the heart he (or she) believes *unto righteousness*, and with the mouth he (or she) confesses unto salvation" (Romans 10:10). Justification is salvation, which is the same thing as believing "unto righteousness." The Agent who gives us the gift of righteousness in justification is the Holy Spirit (compare Romans 8:9, 10 with John 3:3-8).

"In order to meet the requirements of the law, our faith must grasp the righteousness of Christ, accepting it as our righteousness. Through union with Christ, through acceptance of His righteousness by faith, we may be qualified to work the works of God, to be colaborers with Christ. . . . Faith works by love and purifies the soul. Through faith the Holy Spirit works in the heart to create holiness therein; but this cannot be done unless the human agent will work with Christ. We can be fitted for heaven only through the work of the Holy Spirit upon the heart; for we must have Christ's righteousness as our credentials if we would find access to the Father. In order that we may have the righteousness of Christ, we need daily to be transformed by the influence of the Spirit, to be a partaker of the divine nature. It is the work of the Holy Spirit to elevate the taste, to sanctify the heart, to ennoble the whole man" (*Selected Messages*, bk. 1, p. 374).

The point is that justification by faith is reception of the Holy Spirit into our hearts; sanctification is the immediate and long-term result. As the Spirit dwells within, He transforms us in the new-birth experience (justification). He is the Source of our holiness and capacity to demonstrate the character of Jesus (sanctification). This enables us to observe the principles of the divine law (see Romans 8:3, 4).

"Those who know not what it is to have an experience in the things of God, who know not what it is to be justified by faith, who have not the witness of the Spirit that they are accepted of Jesus Christ, are in need of being born again" (*Signs of the Times*, March 8, 1910).

Martin Luther, who "so clearly taught" the doctrine of justification by faith (*The Great Controversy*, p. 253), commented extensively on Galatians 3:2. Notice a little of what he wrote in his 1535 commentary on the book of Galatians:

"Thus: 'You received the Spirit either from the Law or from the hearing of faith. . . . For whatever is not the Holy Spirit or hearing with faith is clearly the Law.' We are dealing here with the issue of justification."

"Then what does justify? Hearing the voice of the Bridegroom, hearing the proclamation of faith—when this is heard, it justifies. Why? Because it brings the Holy Spirit who justifies.

"From this it is sufficiently evident what the distinction is between the Law and the Gospel. The Law never brings the Holy Spirit; therefore it does not justify, because it only teaches what we ought to do. But the Gospel does bring the Holy Spirit, because it teaches what we ought to receive" (*Luther's Works* [St. Louis, Mo.: Concordia, 1963], vol. 26, pp. 203, 208).

Why is it important to identify justification by faith with the new-birth experience? Because the Bible teaches it, and anything taught in the Bible is important. This subject is dealing with the heart of the gospel, the means by which we are saved for eternity. What could be more important? If people gain the impression that salvation or justification is only a legal declaration in heaven quite independent of any transformation of life, they will regard themselves as "saved" even when their characters are out of harmony with the law of God. Such people are divested of spiritual power.

Ellen White explained the point when she wrote of John the Baptist's teaching: "John declared to the Jews that their standing before God was to be decided by their character and life. Profession was worthless. If their life and character were not in harmony with God's law, they were not His people" (*The Desire of Ages*, p. 107). Christ's character becomes ours when we are justified, because then Christ takes up residence in our hearts. As we have observed, this is the message of Paul's epistle to the Romans. Justification is both a legal declaration and heart transformation. God declares righteous the person who receives Christ into his heart by the Holy Spirit.

Righteousness Imputed by the Holy Spirit

Having explained that the gift of the Holy Spirit to the believer is justification, Paul next provides an Old Testament illustration: "Abraham 'believed God, and it was reckoned to him as righteousness' " (Galatians 3:6, RSV). The quotation is from Genesis 15:6. Used by Paul in this context, the verse means that when Abraham received the Spirit by faith, righteousness was reckoned or imputed to him. Justification is imputation [reckoning] of righteousness. This involves the bestowal of the Holy Spirit upon the heart of the believer so that Christ's righteousness becomes his.

Justification equals the gift of the Holy Spirit in the new-birth experience, which equals imputation of righteousness. This is the message of Galatians 3:1-9.

That this is Paul's meaning is supported by his statement a few verses later. Our Lord died for our sins "that in Christ Jesus the blessing of Abraham might come upon the Gentiles, that we might receive the promise of the Spirit through faith" (Galatians 3:14, RSV). Abraham's experience is to be the experience of the believing Gentiles. What was Abraham's experience? The reception of the Holy Spirit into his heart. When Abraham believed, righteousness was reckoned to him because he received the Holy Spirit in justification. In the same manner, the Gentiles believe and receive the imputation of righteousness as the Holy Spirit provides them the new-birth experience.

Martin Luther understood this interpretation of Paul's teaching on imputed righteousness. Commenting on Galatians 2:16, he wrote: "The Christ who is grasped by faith and who lives in the heart is the true Christian righteousness, *on account of which God counts us righteous and grants us eternal life.* . . . Faith takes hold of Christ and has Him present, enclosing Him as the ring encloses the gem. And whoever is found having this faith in the Christ who is grasped in the heart, him God accounts as righteous. . . . Because you have taken hold of Christ by faith, through whom you are righteous, you should now go and love God and your neighbor" (*Luther's Works* [St. Louis, Mo.: Concordia, 1963], vol. 26, pp. 130-133, italics supplied).

Imputed Righteousness in the Epistle to the Romans

The great chapter on imputation of righteousness to the believer is Romans chapter 4. As in the book of Galatians, Paul used Abraham's experience to illustrate justification. Romans 4 was written to illustrate the truth taught in chapter 3:20-31: The righteousness of God is available to the believer not by works of law but by faith (see verses 21, 22). "They are justified by his grace as a gift, through the redemption which is in Christ Jesus" (Romans 3:24, RSV).

The person who has faith receives justification by grace. What is grace? Is it only God's merciful attitude toward us, or is it also His power bestowed upon the believer? Paul answers the question elsewhere: "God is able to make all grace abound toward you; that ye, always having all sufficiency in all things, may abound to every good work" (2 Corinthians 9:8). Grace is a gift to the heart of the believer so that he is able to perform works acceptable to God. Paul wrote to the Corinthians of "the exceeding grace of God *in* you" (2 Corinthians 9:14, italics supplied). He thanked God "for the grace of God which is given you by Jesus Christ; that in every thing ye are enriched by him, in all utterance, and in all knowledge" (1 Corinthians 1:4, 5). Peter urged that we "grow in grace" (2 Peter 3:18).

Grace is the enriching power of God in the life of the believer. Justification is the gift of grace. It is, therefore, the gift of spiritual power to the heart of the believer. This is exactly why Paul wrote that the gospel is *the power of God* unto salvation to every one that believeth" (Romans 1:16, italics supplied). Justification is also the gift of the righteousness of God to the believer (see Romans 1:17; 3:22). Grace, or the righteousness of God, is the power that is bestowed upon our hearts when we are justified. How does this happen? We have already seen that this wonderful gift is ours when, by faith, we receive the Holy Spirit.

Romans chapter 4 is intended to illustrate this truth. Paul

points out that justification is imputation of righteousness, which is forgiveness (see Romans 4:1-8). As demonstrated in an earlier chapter, forgiveness involves two things: (1) Legal abolition of the guilt of our past sins—because of Christ's death for us; (2) "the outflow of redeeming love that transforms the heart" (*Thoughts from the Mount of Blessing*, p. 114). This being the case, when Christ's righteousness is imputed to us, we receive forgiveness involving those two blessings: our guilt is taken away, and we receive "the outflow of redeeming love that transforms the heart."

Then imputation of righteousness must involve a bestowal of righteousness upon the believer by the Holy Spirit. When God imputes righteousness, He does not merely count the sinner righteous in a legal sense. Christ, by the Holy Spirit, takes up residence in the heart.

This truth is supported by Paul's use of Psalm 32:1, 2. Paul quotes: " 'Blessed are those whose iniquities are forgiven, and whose sins are covered; blessed is the man against whom the Lord will not reckon his sin' " (Romans 4:7, 8, RSV). The psalmist adds "and in whose spirit there is no deceit" (Psalm 32:2, RSV). Who is that person? Surely the one who in justification has received the transforming presence of the Holy Spirit. When righteousness is imputed to the believer his spirit is purified because the Holy Spirit has taken possession of his heart.

Imputation in the Old Testament

When Paul used the verb *count* (*reckon, impute*) in Romans 4, he was borrowing an Old Testament term (see Genesis 15:6). The verb *to count* (*reckon, impute*) in both the Hebrew and Greek Old Testaments, sometimes refers to people being regarded as exactly what they are. Nehemiah's treasurers were "counted faithful" because they were faithful (see Nehamiah 13:13). The Emims were counted as giants because they were giants (see Deuteronomy 2:11, 20). Job counted his comforters stupid because they *were* stupid (see Job 18:3). God is never said to count something to be true that is not true.

The verb *count* (*reckon, impute*) sometimes refers to a tangible gift, or statement of ownership. When the tithe was counted (reckoned, imputed) to the Levites, it was given to them. It became their possession (see Numbers 18:26-30). When the town Beeroth was counted (reckoned, imputed) to the tribe of Benjamin, it became the possession of that tribe (see 2 Samuel 4:2).

In the same manner, when righteousness was counted (reckoned, imputed) to Abraham, he was considered to be what the Lord had made him, righteous. This was so because the Lord had bestowed His own righteosness upon him. Abraham believed; God transformed his heart and *simultaneously* declared the reality of His act. The imputation of righteousness (justification) involved both the transformation and the declaration. The declaration was God's recognition of His own presence and power in Abraham's life. Abraham remained a fallen human being with propensities to sin (compare 1 Corinthians 9:27; Galatians 5:17, 18). But as long as Christ dwelt in his life, he retained the blessings of justification.

Ellen G. White's Explanation of Imputed Righteousness

Consistent with Scripture, Ellen G. White identifies imputation of righteousness with justification: "Imputation of the righteousness of Christ comes through justifying faith, and is the justification for which Paul so earnestly contends" (*Selected Messages*, bk. 1, p. 397).

Consistent with Scripture, Ellen G. White explains the imputation of righteousness in two ways:

1. *The righteousness of Christ is put to the believer's account.* "Christ's righteousness is accepted in place of man's failure, and God receives, pardons, justifies, the repentant, believing soul, treats him as though he were righteous, and loves him as He loves His Son. This is how faith is accounted righteousness" (*Selected Messages*, bk. 1, p. 367).

2. *When righteousness is imputed to the believer, Christ's righteousness is bestowed upon him by the Holy Spirit.* "By receiving His imputed righteousness, through the transform-

ing power of the Holy Spirit, we become like Him" (*SDA Bible Commentary*, vol. 6, p. 1098).

"In ourselves we are sinners; but in Christ we are righteous. Having made us righteous through the imputed righteousness of Christ, God pronounces us just, and treats us as just" (*Selected Messages*, bk. 1, p. 394).

"He has become sin for us that we might become the righteousness of God in Him. Through faith in His name He imputes unto us His righteousness, and it becomes a living principle in our life" (*That I May Know Him*, p. 302).

"Let perfect obedience be rendered to God through the imputed righteousness of Christ, and we shall reveal to the world the fact that God loves us as he loves Jesus" (*Signs of the Times*, May 28, 1896).

"His righteousness He would impute to man, and thus raise him in moral value with God, so that his efforts to keep the divine law would be acceptable. Christ's work was to reconcile man to God through His human nature, and God to man through His divine nature" (*Selected Messages*, bk. 1, p. 273).

Summary

Galatians 3:1-9 identifies justification with the transforming work of the Holy Spirit in the life of the believer. Paul speaks of justification as imputation of righteousness, pointing out that the blessing of righteousness by faith given to Abraham can be ours, because we can "receive the promise of the Spirit through faith" (Galatians 3:14).

Chapter 6
Jesus Only—Always

Galatians 3:10-18

During a visit to Pacific Union College a few years before his death, Elder H. M. S. Richards, Sr., the founder and director of the Voice of Prophecy, was interviewed on the college radio station. The young man conducting the interview questioned, "Elder Richards, if you were asked to summarize the gospel in one sentence, how would you answer?" Without hesitation, Elder Richards responded, "Jesus only."

What a delightfully biblical response! And how relevant to the universal need of humanity! Elder Richards meant that there is no other workable solution to the human sin problem. Some people use drugs or alcohol to blot out the ugly areas of life and to reverse their hurtful, negative responses. Others resort to psychologists and psychiatrists in an attempt to be relieved of their feelings of guilt and their overwhelming compulsion to sin. They may receive some help, but the basic problem remains. Yet others immerse themselves in entertainment, illicit sex, or even work, as the means of escape from the bitter realities of life. But the record is still there, and the immovable tendency to evil urges them inexorably to modes of behavior that, in their inmost heart, they despise. "All have sinned, and come short of the glory of God" (Romans 3:23). "The carnal mind is enmity against God: for it is not subject to the law of God, neither indeed can be" (Romans 8:7).

Some Christians try to bury their guilt by strenuous attempts to earn God's good will. By unreasonably strict adherence to the minutiae of religious life, they salve their consciences and effectively ignore "the weightier matters of the law, judgment, mercy, and faith" (Matthew 23:23). Other Christians go to the opposite extreme of ignoring God's law, imagining that, because they are saved by grace, they are safe in Christ's hands, despite their occasional or habitual capitulation to the clamorings of their fallen natures.

The only ultimate answer to our deepest spiritual and psychological needs is provided by Jesus. Truth is a Person, not merely a philosophy or a way of life—even though the correct teaching and the correct way of life are inseparable from the Person of the Saviour. Only as we reach out by faith and receive Jesus into our hearts can we achieve the divinely ordained purpose for our existence. Peace of mind and spiritual fulfillment reside only in union with Jesus Christ.

This is the burden of Paul's message in the Galatian epistle. Deliverance from our conflicts and sins, and ultimate joy in the kingdom of heaven are available only by a faith-grace union with One who bore our guilt on the cross. Jesus is always the only answer!

The verses studied in this chapter are Galatians 3:10-18. Four questions are answered in this study: (1) Why the curse? (2) Who are the just? (3) How did Christ redeem us? (4) Has Jesus always been the only answer?

Why the Curse?

"As many as are of the works of the law are under the curse: for it is written, Cursed is every one that continueth not in all things which are written in the book of the law to do them." "The law is not of faith: but, The man that doeth them shall live in them" (Galatians 3:10, 12).

Anyone who breaks God's law is under the curse of condemnation. Because the divine law is a standard of righteousness, anyone who fails to adhere to the standard is condemned to eternal death. That is the consistent teaching of Scripture (see Romans 6:23).

As a means of testing whether Adam and Eve would be willing to live consistently by the principles of His government, God placed the tree of knowedge of good and evil in the garden of Eden. He said, "In the day that thou eatest thereof thou shalt surely die" (Genesis 2:17). God's will was the standard of righteousness. Acting contrary to His will would inevitably result in eternal death. Our first parents ate of the forbidden tree, broke the divine standard, and brought sin and death into the world. The curse came upon them and their children because of sin.

Paul discusses the results of sin in Romans 5:12-21. He introduces the subject with an incomplete sentence: "Therefore as sin came into the world through one man and death through sin, and so death spread to all men because all men sinned" (Romans 5:12, RSV). Sin is a curse that results in the curse of death. Why did death come upon all humanity? Paul answers in verse 18: "Then as one man's trespass led to condemnation for all men."

Years ago I read that text to a lady with whom I was having a Bible study. "That's unjust!" she reacted. "Why should the whole world be cursed with condemnation to eternal death because of one man's sin?"

Now that is a good question. Were the inhabitants of earth treated as guilty of what Adam and Eve committed? The Bible answers, No. "The soul that sins shall die" (Ezekial 18:20, RSV). Then why should all be condemned for the sin of our first parents?

Perhaps an illustration will help. A child born of parents who have AIDS will probably have the disease; yet the child is not guilty of any sin that the parents, or anyone else, may have committed. The child is condemned to have the disease, but is not guilty of anyone else's sin. In a similar way, every human being has been born with a disease, a fallen nature that is prone to sin because our first parents chose to disobey God. We were not born guilty, but we were born fallen. Fallen human beings cannot live eternally with God unless they are willing to allow Him to transform their natures. That is why Jesus said, "Ye must be born again" (John 3:7).

The opportunity to be changed and delivered from condemnation has been available to everyone who has ever lived.

Jesus was the "Lamb slain from the foundation of the world" (Revelation 13:8). This is why in Romans 5:12-21 Paul consistently points us to the sacrifice of Christ for all humanity. Believing in Christ, anyone can find redemption from the results of Adam's fall. No one has to be lost eternally because of the dominance of a fallen nature.

The curse resulting from Adam's sin is the fallen, sinful nature with which we all were born. Because we inherit this nature with its biases toward evil, it was natural for us to choose sin. But what was natural was not essential. At every stage of history God has provided a way of escape through Christ. We did not have to commit sin; it was not an imperative. But we chose to do it because we were not willing to rely on God for the victory. When we made that choice, we incurred guilt of our own. Then we came under condemnation to eternal death because of our own acts of sin. Only by accepting Jesus could we be forgiven and transformed.

Paul explains in Galatians 3:10, 12 that all those who depend on their own efforts to keep the law as a means of salvation from sin are placing themselves back under the curse of the law. They are placing their own works ahead of Christ's works. His work on the cross delivers us from sin and death. When we rely on our efforts instead of His, we effectively neutralize the only means by which God can save us. Once again we are under the dominance of our fallen natures with no power to overcome sin; once again we are condemned to death by the law we have broken.

Paul quotes two Old Testament passages to illustrate his point. The first is Deuteronomy 27:26: " 'Cursed be he who does not confirm the words of this law by doing them' " (RSV). The second comes from Leviticus 18:5: " 'You shall therefore keep my statutes and my ordinances, by doing which a man shall live: I am the Lord your God' " (RSV). These two commands to ancient Israel were to be obeyed by faith in God. In the context of the books of Moses, the command to obey the law always implied that it was to be done by reliance upon the covenant relationship with Jehovah. Consider, for example, the injunction of Deuteronomy 6:5, 6: " 'You shall love the

Lord your God with all your heart, and with all your soul, and with all your might. And these words which I command you this day shall be upon your heart' " (RSV). Obedience based on a love relationship with God, in which He writes the law on the heart of the believer, is the essence of righteousness by faith (see Romans 10:6-10). This faith-grace, covenant relationship is emphasized throughout the Pentateuch (compare Deuteronomy 30:11-14). Circumcision of the heart, a spiritual transformation resulting from a personal union with God, was essential for the Israelite who wished to obey God's law (see Deuteronomy 10:16; 30:6).

In Galatians 3:10, 12, Paul separates the *principle* of obedience from the *means* of obedience. He demonstrates that, without the latter (a faith-grace union with God), a person is bound to fail. If you take the two Old Testament commands Paul quotes and attempt to live by them, without entering into a relationship with Christ, you place yourself back under the curse of sin and condemnation. Present obedience cannot atone for past sin, even if it were possible without Christ. The fact is that without His control in our lives, we are the victims of sin. The person who depends upon his own works for salvation cannot enjoy Christ's controlling presence.

Who Are the Just?

"That no man is justified by the law in the sight of God, it is evident: for, The just shall live by faith" (Galatians 3:11). The principle comes from the Old Testament; the quotation is from Habakkuk 2:4. The Revised Standard Version translates Paul's sentence: " 'He who through faith is righteous shall live.' " The Greek reads more simply: "The righteous person shall live by faith."

"The just" is "the righteous person." Such a person is righteous because of faith in Christ. In what sense is this person righteous? It is instructive to consider the context of the same statement in the book of Romans. "I am not ashamed of the gospel: it is the power of God for salvation to every one who has faith, to the Jew first and also to the Greek. *For in it the righteousness of God is revealed* through faith for faith; as it is written, 'He who through faith is righteous shall live' " (Romans 1:16, 17, RSV, italics supplied).

The gospel is "the power of God unto salvation to every one that believeth," because in it is "the righteousness of God revealed." The verb *reveal* (Greek, *apokalupto*) means "show," "disclose," "bring to light," "uncover." Sometimes in the New Testament this word refers to the light of truth—the knowledge of God revealed to minds and hearts by the Holy Spirit. Such revealed divine knowledge is not mere factual information; it is a spiritual experience by which truth becomes part of a life; it is a bestowal of spiritual power that the believer experiences. The gospel is the power of God to the believer because he experiences the righteousness of God. He does not merely know that God is righteous; he takes into his life the transforming power of God's righteousness.

The same verb *reveal* is used in Paul's first letter to the Corinthians. "As it is written, 'What no eye has seen, nor ear heard, nor the heart of man conceived, what God has prepared for those who love him,' God *has revealed* to us through the Spirit. For the Spirit searches everything, even the depths of God" (1 Corinthians 2:9, 10, RSV, italics supplied). The passage that Paul is quoting from the Old Testament (see Isaiah 64:4) is applied to the kingdom state in its original setting. Paul applies it to the present. He emphasizes that, because of the teaching ministry of the Holy Spirit in our hearts, divine mysteries are revealed to us now. The revelation is a spiritual experience resulting from the indwelling of the Holy Spirit.

Jesus thanked His Father that He had hidden certain truths " 'from the wise and understanding and *revealed* them to babes' " (Matthew 11:25, RSV, italics supplied). He added, " 'All things have been delivered to me by my Father; and no one knows the Son except the Father, and no one knows the Father except the Son and any one to whom the Son chooses *to reveal* him' " (Matthew 11:27, RSV, italics supplied). Once again the revelation is to the heart of the humble believer.

When Paul wrote that the gospel is power for the believer because in it is the "righteousness of God revealed," he meant that God's righteousness is bestowed upon you when you accept Christ. Christ is not asking you only to admire His personal righteousness. He is inviting you to take it into your heart. The divine revelation of righteousness to the heart of the believer is the power that transforms him from a habitual sinner to a habitual servant of Christ. This is the power that qualifies a person for heaven. This is why Paul craved to "be found in him, not having mine own righteousness, which is of the law, but that which is through the faith of Christ, the righteousness which is of God by faith" (Philippians 3:9).

Then is the believer in Christ righteous? If this question means: "Is the believer independently righteous in soul, so that now he can go it alone without total dependence on Christ for victory over sin and the daily power to live for God?" the answer is an emphatic "No!" On the other hand, if we are asking: "Is the believer righteous because Christ is righteous, and Christ is daily bestowing His righteousness upon him?" the answer is a resounding "Yes!"

The apostle John supplemented Paul's discussion of this subject: "If you know that He is righteous, you know that every one who does righteousness has been born of Him" (1 John 2:29, literal translation). The born-again Christian is given the power to do works that God regards as righteous. John warned: "Little children, let no one deceive you; he who does righteousness is righteous, as he is righteous" (1 John 3:7, RSV). As we have discovered, because Christ comes into our hearts by the Holy Spirit, we have His righteous presence (see Romans 8:9, 10). In this sense we have righteousness.

How Did Christ Redeem Us?

"Christ hath redeemed us from the curse of the law, being made a curse for us" (Galatians 3:13). He bore the curse of human guilt and condemnation. He took upon Himself that which was ours, so that we might take upon us that which is His. "For our sake he made him to be sin who knew no sin, so that in him we might become the righteousness of God" (2 Corinthians 5:21, RSV). The Greek verb translated *become* in the last phrase is often used as the equivalent of the verb *to be.* Christ took our sin, "so that we might *be* the righteousness of God in Him."

"Christ was treated as we deserve, that we might be treated as He deserves. He was condemned for our sins, in which He had no share, that we might be justified by His righteousness, in which we had no share. He suffered the death which was ours, that we might receive the life which was His. 'With His stripes we are healed' " (*The Desire of Ages*, p. 25).

We know that when Christ bore our guilt on the cross, He was not merely counted to be a sinner without any of the accompanying suffering that accrues to the one separated from God. "He himself *bore our sins in his body on the tree*, that we might die to sin and live to righteousness" (1 Peter 2:24, RSV, italics supplied). Just as Christ, treated as a sinner though thoroughly innocent, suffered in Himself the intense results of human guilt, so we, treated as righteous though thoroughly guilty, experience the thrill of taking upon ourselves His righteousness as the Holy Spirit brings His presence to our hearts.

Has Jesus Always Been the Only Answer?

Paul's legalistic opponents in Galatia were suggesting that the law God gave to His people at Sinai should be used as the means of salvation. They implied that their efforts to obey both the moral and ceremonial laws resulted in righteousness, acceptance with God, and a place in His kingdom.

Paul answered by pointing out that when the Lord proclaimed His law from Sinai, He in no way intended to destroy the terms of the covenant that He had made with Abraham 430 years earlier. Paul pointed out that a legal covenant between two people or a human will would never be changed without the permission of the people who originally signed it. Just so, God's will, His agreement with Abraham, was not changed in any particular when the law was given at Sinai (see Galatians 3:15-17).

What was the Lord's agreement with Abraham? He said in effect, "Abraham, you trust Me, and I will give you a son in your old age, and the Messiah will be one of your direct descendants" (see Genesis 12:3; Galatians 3:8; John 8:56). The Lord added, "Abraham, you believe in the Messiah to come, and I will give you the gift of My righteousness by the Holy Spirit (see Genesis 15:1-6; Galatians 3:6, 14). The Lord also said, "Abraham, you believe in Me, and I will give you and your descendants the land of Canaan as a token of the heavenly Canaan that you will inherit at the second coming of Jesus" (see Genesis 17:7, 8; Hebrews 11:10).

The Messiah, His righteousness for those who have faith, and the heavenly land—these same three major promises were valid from Sinai till the cross. They were not abolished or even modified by the giving of the law at Sinai. Hence, those who argue that, although now we are saved by grace, before the cross people were saved by obedience to the law, are teaching an unbiblical doctrine. Israelites were saved by grace at every stage of their history. Christ was just as much the answer to their need as He was the answer to Abraham's need and as He is to ours.

The ten-commandment law was given at Sinai as the standard of righteousness for all ages of history (see Romans 3:31; 7:7, 12, 14; 8:3, 4). The Lord intends us to keep it by faith in Jesus. His infinite power is made available to every person who will receive His divine presence and righteousness by the Holy Spirit. This person responds positively to Jesus' command: " 'If you love me, you will keep my commandments' " (John 14:15, RSV).

Summary

The curse of the law from which we are redeemed when we trust in Jesus is the guilt and condemnation that we have incurred by disobeying God. When we try to make ourselves righteous by our own efforts to obey, we inevitably fall and place ourselves under that curse. Jesus bore our guilt on the cross so that we can receive His righteousness by the gift of the Holy Spirit. This wonderful gift enables us to obey His law.

Chapter 7
Why Does God Have Laws?

Galatians 3:19, 20

As a graduate assistant in the speech department of Michigan State University in 1963, one of my responsibilities was to evaluate the speeches of undergraduate students. Actions may speak louder than words, but in this process the words of the students were most revealing. Some of them were eloquent in their defense of teenage drinking, premarital sex, coed dormitories, elimination of grades for college students, and a host of other things that society at that time regarded as contrary to accepted norms of behavior. The prevailing argument of many students was that if only certain laws could be abolished there would be less crime. They argued that the very existence of the laws induced young people to break them. The joy of law breaking would not exist if the laws did not exist.

This attitude to law is quite prevalent today. Some time ago United Press International reported: "More and more, law enforcement officials are coming around to the conclusion that the only way to reduce the crime rate in America is to make everything legal.

"Moves in various parts of the country to decriminalize marijuana are illustrative of this approach. If adopted nationwide, proponents claim, decriminalization would produce a dramatic decline in the number of arrests for illegal pot possession.

"There is also talk of employing the legalization technique to stamp out violations of laws against pornography, prostitution, gambling and assorted other vices.

"One of the leading advocates of decriminalization is an organization called Less Lawlessness Through Less Law (LLLL).

" 'Hiring more policemen, imposing curfews, building new prisons, enlarging the judiciary—these measures only treat the symptoms of the crime wave,' Bargood Fie, a LLLL spokesman, told me.

" 'If we're ever going to have a genuine improvement in the situation we've got to attack the root cause of crime—the laws' " (quoted in *Encyclopedia of 7700 Illustrations* [Rockville, Md.: Assurance Publishers, 1988], p. 725).

The apostle Paul was accused of a similar attitude to law. He was preaching with eloquence and vigor that salvation is by faith (grace) alone. Works of law, he maintained, do not recommend a sinner to Christ, nor do they wipe out guilt for past sins. Only as the sinner comes by faith, accepting Christ's sacrifice, confessing his own sin and repenting of it, can he be forgiven and have the gifts of righteousness and eternal life.

Paul's legalistic Jewish opponents thought he was reducing the culpability of the sinner by abolishing the law. They responded, "If salvation is by faith alone, why did God take the trouble to proclaim His law from Mount Sinai? If, as Paul insists, the covenant made with Abraham involved righteousness and salvation by faith alone, and this covenant was not modified in any way by the giving the law at Sinai 430 years later (see Galatians 3:15-18), why did God give the law?"

Anticipating the question, Paul raised it himself in his epistle to the Galatians. "Why then the law? It was added because of transgressions, till the offspring should come to whom the promise had been made; and it was ordained by angels through an intermediary. Now an intermediary implies more than one; but God is one" (Galatians 3:19, 20, RSV).

"It Was Added"

The law was "added" at Sinai 430 years after the Lord

made the covenant with Abraham. Righteousness and salvation were given to Abraham because of his faith in the Messiah. When God gave Moses the law for His people at Sinai, He did not change the Abrahamic covenant (see Galatians 3:15-18). He offered the same covenant promises to Israel.

Among the words that the Lord communicated through Moses to the people were these: " 'Now therefore, if you will obey my voice and keep *my covenant*, you shall be my own possession among all peoples; for all the earth is mine, and you shall be to me a kingdom of priests and a holy nation' " (Exodus 19:5, 6, RSV, italics supplied). What did the Lord mean by "my covenant"? He meant the same covenant that He gave to Abraham. He had approached Abraham centuries before, saying, " 'I will establish *my covenant* between me and you and your descendants after you throughout their generations for an everlasting covenant, to be God to you and to your descendants after you' " (Genesis 17:7, RSV, italics supplied; compare verses 9, 19).

God's covenant offered to Israel at Sinai was the same one that He had offered to Abraham "He is mindful of his covenant for ever, of the word that he commanded, for a thousand generations, the covenant which he made with Abraham, his sworn promise to Isaac, which he confirmed to Jacob as a statute, to Israel as an everlasting covenant" (Psalm 105:8-10).

The terms of this covenant have always been God's means of salvation for lost humanity. He offers the same terms to us today:

"The covenant that God made with His people at Sinai is to be our refuge and defense. . . .

" 'And Moses came and called for the elders of the people, and laid before their faces all these words.'

" 'And all the people answered together, and said, All that the Lord hath spoken we will do.'

"This covenant is of just as much force today as it was when the Lord made it with ancient Israel" (*SDA Bible Commentary,* vol. 1, p. 1103).

"The Lord made a special covenant with his ancient Israel if they would prove faithful . . . [Exodus 19:5, 6 quoted]. And he thus addresses his commandment-keeping people in these last days" (Ellen G. White, *Review and Herald*, September 7, 1886).

The Lord offered Israel, and He offers us, exactly the same terms that He offered Abraham—righteousness and salvation by faith in Christ. The adding of the law at Sinai did not change God's promises to the one who has faith. The law is an integral part of God's covenant. When giving the covenant to Abraham, God said: "Walk before me, and be thou perfect" (Genesis 17:1). Despite his numerous sins and mistakes, by faith Abraham obeyed that command. "Abraham obeyed my voice and kept my charge, my commandments, my statutes, and my laws" (Genesis 26:5, RSV). When God made that statement He was focusing on the trend of Abraham's life, which was habitual obedience by faith. When Abraham fell into sin, he always repented and renewed his covenant relationship with God. And that relationship was the source of his power to overcome.

The law of God had always existed; it did not originate at Sinai. At Creation, God gave Adam and Eve the Sabbath command (see Genesis 2:1-3). The Sabbath command given at Sinai was a reiteration of the law that had existed all along. We are to " 'remember the sabbath day, to keep it holy; . . . for in six days the Lord made heaven and earth, the sea, and all that is in them, and rested the seventh day; therefore the Lord blessed the sabbath day and hallowed it' " (Exodus 20:8-11, RSV).

By faith Abraham obeyed the moral law of God that had always existed as the basis of God's government. The same law was spelled out at Sinai. Even the ceremonial law existed in embryo from the time when our first parents fell into sin. "By faith Abel offered to God a more acceptable sacrifice than Cain, through which he received approval as righteous" (Hebrews 11:4, RSV). The patriarchs from Abel to Sinai regularly offered animal sacrifices to God as an indication of their faith in the Messiah to come. The sacrificial system given immediately after the Fall was the gospel in type.

"The law of God existed before the creation of man or else Adam could not have sinned. After the transgression of Adam the principles of the law were not changed, but were definitely arranged and expressed to meet man in his fallen condition. Christ, in counsel with His Father, instituted the system of sacrificial offerings; that death, instead of being immediately visited upon the transgressor, should be transferred to a victim which should prefigure the great and perfect offering of the Son of God" (*Selected Messages*, bk. 1, p. 230).

Thus the Sinai law added to the Abrahamic covenant was a specific formulation of that law that had always existed. There is nothing specifically Jewish about God's law. The Ten Commandments are an expression of the eternal principles which form the basis of God's government. The ceremonial law given at Sinai was an expansion of the sacrificial system that had been in operation since the fall of our first parents into sin.

The terms of the covenant offered Israel at Sinai were the same as those that had been offered to fallen mankind ever since the time of Adam. The law, moral and ceremonial, added in a written form at Sinai, expressed the principles by which God had intended mankind to live from the beginnings of human history.

"Because of Transgressions"

Why was the written form of the law added at Sinai? Paul answers: "It was added because of transgressions" (Galatians 3:19). This is another way of saying that the law was given at Sinai for the express purpose of convincing the people of Israel that they were sinners in need of a Saviour. They had just come out of slavery in Egypt. Imagine how difficult it must have been for the Israelite slaves to remember the principles of God's law that had been handed down by word of mouth from one patriarch to another! They had become degraded by servitude and exposure to the idolatrous and intemperate practices of their Egyptian overlords.

How could the Lord awaken these poor, darkened minds to the holy principles by which He wanted them to live? How better than by leading them through difficult experiences designed to build their faith in Him. How better than by presenting the principles of His government in a dramatic exhibition of His power.

"Moreover the law entered, that the offence might abound. But where sin abounded, grace did much more abound" (Romans 5:20). J. B. Phillips paraphrases this verse as follows: "Now we find that the Law keeps slipping into the picture to point the vast extent of sin" (*Letters to Young Churches*). Israel became aware of the vast extent of their sin when they saw God's standard of righteousness in relation to their own moral degradation. They were condemned by the Ten Commandments and were pointed to Christ as their only hope of salvation. They took courage as they offered animal sacrifices that represented the sacrifice He was to make for them.

In his letter to the Romans, Paul rejoiced that the law continues to function: "If it had not been for the law, I should not have known sin. I should not have known what it is to covet if the law had not said, 'You shall not covet.' . . . Apart from the law sin lies dead. I was once alive apart from the law, but when the commandment came, sin revived and I died; the very commandment which promised life proved to be death to me. For sin, finding opportunity in the commandment, deceived me and by it killed me. So the law is holy, and the commandment is holy and just and good" (Romans 7:7-12, RSV).

The law that condemned Paul to death also pointed him to the means of eternal life. "Wretched man that I am! Who will deliver me from this body of death? Thanks be to God through Jesus Christ our Lord" (Romans 7:24, 25, RSV). And the law does this for *us*, also. We see in Jesus our perfectly righteous Lord whose life is the exemplification of the principles of His own law. We see in Him our sacrifice, our heavenly Mediator, our indwelling righteousness, our means of victory over sin, and our eternal Saviour. "Thanks be unto God for his unspeakable gift" (2 Corinthians 9:15).

"Till the Seed Should Come"

"Wherefore then serveth the law? It was added because of transgressions, till the seed should come to whom the promise was made" (Galatians 3:19). The New International Version translates the text this way: "It was added because of transgressions until the Seed to whom the promise referred had come." Another possible translation is: ". . . till the Seed should come concerning whom the promise was made."

The Seed is Christ. Paul has already made that point. "He saith not, And to seeds, as of many; but as of·one, And to thy seed, which is Christ" (Galatians 3:16). So the written form of the law given at Sinai was until the coming of Christ.

Does this imply that when Christ came the law ceased to exist? As we have already seen, Paul explained to the Roman Christians how the law had pointed out his sin after the cross (see Romans 7:7-14). He consistently emphasized that Christ died "in order that the righteous requirements of the law might be fully met in us, who do not live according to the sinful nature but according to the Spirit" (Romans 8:4, NIV). If the law's requirements are to be fulfilled in us, the law continues to function as God's standard of righteousness.

Paul is in perfect agreement with Jesus and the apostles. Jesus taught: "Think not that I am come to destroy the law, or the prophets: I am not come to destroy, but to fulfil. For verily I say unto you, Till heaven and earth pass, one jot or one tittle shall in no wise pass from the law, till all be fulfilled. Whosoever therefore shall break one of these least commandments, and shall teach men so, he shall be called the least in the kingdom of heaven" (Matthew 5:17-19; compare 1 John 2:2-4; James 1:22-25; 2:8-12; Revelation 12:17; 14:12).

Nothing could be clearer. The law still functions as Christ's standard of righteousness because heaven and earth still exist. The moral law of ten commandments expresses righteous principles that were the basis of God's government in the eternal ages before Creation and that will continue as such for eternity in the future.

But what about the ceremonial law that was added at Sinai? Did Jesus mean to imply that it should be kept after His death? Indeed, no! The system of sacrifices and offerings in the ceremonial law were the gospel before the death of Jesus. When Jesus died and rose again, the sacrifices did not need to be offered any more, because the event to which they had pointed had occurred (see Ephesians 2:14-17; Hebrews 9:1-14; 10:1-14).

Because the ceremonial law was done away with at the

cross, while the moral law of ten commandments continues to function, would we be correct to assume that Galatians 3:19 is referring only to the ceremonial law? Is this alone the law that was added at Sinai? The context of the passage answers the question. The law that was given 430 years after the covenant made with Abraham was not only the ceremonial law (see Galatians 3:17). It was both the Ten Commandments and the ceremonial law. The law that cannot provide for the faithful an eternal inheritance (see Galatians 3:18), that cannot make us spiritually alive by giving us righteousness (verse 21) is not only the ceremonial law; it is also the moral law of ten commandments. The law that is "our schoolmaster to bring us unto Christ" (Galatians 3:24) is not only the ceremonial law but also the ten-commandment law. Paul's whole point in the epistle to the Galatians is that righteousness and salvation are not earned by obedience to any law, moral or ceremonial. They are Christ's gift to the one who has faith.

Hence, when Paul asked, "Why then the law?" he meant, "Why was the law, both moral and ceremonial, given at Sinai?" Ellen G. White explained: "I am asked concerning the law in Galatians. What law is the schoolmaster to bring us to Christ? I answer: Both the ceremonial and the moral code of ten commandments. . . .

" 'The law was our schoolmaster to bring us unto Christ, that we might be justified by faith' " (Galatians 3:24). In this scripture, the Holy Spirit through the apostle is speaking especially of the moral law. The law reveals sin to us, and causes us to feel our need of Christ and to flee unto Him for pardon and peace by exercising repentance toward God and faith toward our Lord Jesus Christ.

"An unwillingness to yield up preconceived opinions, and to accept this truth, lay at the foundation of a large share of the opposition manifested at Minneapolis against the Lord's message through Brethren [E. J.] Waggoner and [A. T.] Jones. By exciting that opposition Satan succeeded in shutting away from our people, in a great measure, the special power of the Holy Spirit that God longed to impart to them. The enemy prevented them from obtaining that efficiency which might have been theirs in carrying the truth to the world, as the apostles proclaimed it after the day of Pentecost. The light that is to lighten the whole earth with its glory was resisted, and by the action of our own brethren has been in a great degree kept away from the world" (*Selected Messages*, bk. 1, pp. 233-235).

Since the law that was added at Sinai includes the Ten Commandments, which continue to function after the cross as the standard of righteousness, why did Paul write that the law "was added" *"till the seed should come"* (Galatians 3:19, italics supplied)? The word *till* is not intended to suggest that the law was abolished at the cross. Paul wrote to Timothy, *"Till* I come, give attendance to reading, to exhortation, to doctrine" (1 Timothy 4:13, italics supplied). Obviously that did not mean that after Paul's arrival Timothy could cease reading, exhorting, and teaching. Jesus instructs us, "Hold fast *till* I come" (Revelation 2:25, italics supplied). Of course, we will continue to hold fast after He comes. The word *till* does not imply a time limit for the action mentioned in the sentence. Likewise, when Paul wrote that the law was added "till the seed should come" he did not mean that the law would cease to function after the Seed had come. Even the principles of the ceremonial law continue to be applied in the High Priest ministry of Christ for His believing people.

Even so, the phrase "till the seed should come" seems to imply that the moral law functioned somewhat differently before the time of Jesus from the manner in which it does after that time. Would such a conclusion be valid? We will answer that question in our next chapter.

Summary

Because Paul emphasized righteousness by faith alone, it was logical for his readers to ask, What is the purpose of the law? Why was it given? Paul answered that the law in the form in which it was given at Sinai was designed to point out sin and direct sinners to Christ. Although it continues to perform these functions today, there is a suggestion in Galatians 3:19 that perhaps the law functioned somewhat differently before the cross. This is the subject of our next chapter.

Chapter 8
How God Prepared the World for the Coming of Christ

Galatians 3:21-25

"Two close friends, a Jew and a Christian, often discussed their religions. Finally they decided to visit each other's place of worship. They went to the synagogue first. The time for the offering came, and the Jew took a check out of his pocket and placed it in the offering plate. The Christian was very inquisitive and wanted to see the figure on that check. So he wiggled and wiggled until he caught sight of it. He immediately turned to his Jewish friend and said, 'Abe, is this your weekly or your monthly offering?'

"Abe turned to his Christian friend and said, 'Why, don't you know I am an orthodox Jew and the Old Testament tells me that I should give one tenth of all that I make to the Lord? I thought you Christians did exactly the same thing.'

" 'Oh, no,' the Christian replied. 'Don't you know that we have been emancipated from the law and we are now under grace. We are free people; we are not bound by this law or any other.'

" 'And what do you do when it comes to your offerings to the church?'

" 'Oh, Abe, that is simple. At the end of the week, we just give what is left over.'

" 'Really,' Abraham answered with surprise, 'thou almost doth persuade me to become a Christian' " (*Pulpit Helps*, July 1989, p. 14).

"Sin shall not have dominion over you: for ye are not under the law, but under grace" (Romans 6:14). The Christian young man presented to his Jewish friend a sad distortion of Paul's meaning. Paul did not mean to imply that we are now free from the obligation to obey God's law. "Do we then make void the law through faith? God forbid: yea, we establish the law" (Romans 3:31). Paul meant that because we are under grace we are not under law keeping as the *means of attaining righteousness and salvation*. Because we are under grace as the means of power and victory over sin, we are not living in sin, under the law's condemnation. Romans 6:15 is revealing: "What then? shall we sin, because we are not under the law, but under grace? God forbid." Sin is "transgression of the law" (1 John 3:4). That being so, the person under grace who is not sinning is living in obedience to God's law.

What is God's law? Every divine command in Scripture, except those that specifically met their fulfillment at the cross. The tithing principle that the Jewish young man was practicing has universal application for all time (compare Malachi 3:7-12; 1 Corinthians 9:13, 14). The Ten Commandments, given their more strict interpretation by Jesus (see Matthew 5), remain as God's great standard of righteousness (see Romans 7:7, 12, 14; 8:3, 4).

Yet Seventh-day Adventists are often regarded as legalists because they appropriate the gift of God's grace as the power to obey God's law. We are told that the fourth commandment, the Sabbath commandment, no longer has validity, because the Ten Commandments were a "schoolmaster" only until Christ came (see Galatians 3:24, 25).

Years ago, at the age of nineteen, I was a student colporteur in Melbourne, Australia. At one house a woman and her little girl came to the door, and I proceeded to present the canvass for the books I was selling. Quickly realizing that I was a Seventh-day Adventist, the woman came right to the point. She said, "You know, you Adventists are wrong on the law.

You are contradicting grace because you insist on keeping the Ten Commandments." She invited me to a Bible study in her home a few nights later, and we sat up till late, discussing Bible teaching. The passage that she kept presenting to me as evidence against the need to keep the Sabbath was Galatians 3:21-25. All my efforts to convince her of the true meaning of the passage were unavailing.

Does the Law Oppose the Gospel?

"Is the law then against the promises of God? God forbid: for if there had been a law given which could have given life, verily righteousness should have been by the law" (Galatians 3:21).

The law is not antagonistic to God's promises. It is not at all opposed to the gospel. This is the message of the preceding verses. Speaking of the covenant to Abraham and the giving of the law at Sinai 430 years later, Paul explained: "This is what I mean: the law, which came four hundred and thirty years afterward, does not annul a covenant previously ratified by God, so as to make the promise void" (Galatians 3:17, RSV). Because the giving of the law did not change the covenant promises of righteousness and eternal life to those who have faith, the law cannot be said to contradict the promises of God.

The law is not against the gospel of salvation by faith alone; the law is against sin. When we sin, the law reveals it to us and drives us to Christ as the great Source of forgiveness and cleansing. "If it had not been for the law, I should not have known sin. I should not have known what it is to covet if the law had not said, 'You shall not covet'" (Romans 7:7, RSV).

James illustrated the same process. He likened the law to a mirror (see James 1:22-25). Some people with dirty faces look into a miror but do not correct the problem by washing. Others act immediately and wash the dirt away. "But he who looks into the perfect law, the law of liberty, and perseveres, being no hearer that forgets but a doer that acts, he shall be blessed in his doing" (James 1:25, RSV).

What is this law of liberty? "Whoever keeps the whole law but fails in one point has become guilty of all of it. For he who said, 'Do not commit adultery,' said also, 'Do not kill.' If you do not commit adultery but do kill, you have become a transgressor of the law. So speak and so act as those who are to be judged under the law of liberty" (James 2:10-12, RSV). The law of liberty is the law James has quoted: the Ten Commandments. The fourth commandment, the Sabbath command, is just as important as the commands against adultery and killing. Because James says that the person who breaks one of God's commands is guilty of breaking the whole law, the person who does not observe the Sabbath is a lawbreaker.

How does James recommend that we keep the law of liberty, the Ten Commandments? "Faith by itself, if it has no works, is dead. . . . I by my works will show you my faith" (James 2:17, 18, RSV). We keep the law of liberty by having living faith. This is faith that works; it is faith that does what God asks (compare Galatians 5:6). The works of obedience to God's law demonstrate that they have been produced by living faith exercised by the totally committed Christian.

Although the law of God is obeyed by those who have living faith, it does not have the power to "make alive" (Galatians 3:21, RSV). We are not made righteous by the law. Spiritual life with Christ, involving His righteousness in the heart by the presence of the Holy Spirit, is a promise of God, bestowed as a gift of His grace to the one who has faith. The law was never intended to make us righteous. "God has done *what the law*, weakened by the flesh, *could not do*: sending his own Son in the likeness of sinful flesh and for sin, he condemned sin in the flesh, in order *that the just requirement of the law might be fulfilled in us*, who walk not according to the flesh but according to the Spirit" (Romans 8:3, 4, RSV, italics supplied).

The law condemns the sinner to death and points him to Christ. Only Jesus can forgive, purify from sin, bestow righteousness, bring the believer into complete conformity to the principles of His law, and reserve him or her for eternal life (see John 3:36; 1 John 5:10-14).

When Paul said, "The scripture hath concluded all under sin" (Galatians 3:22), he meant that the law has condemned everyone to eternal death because everyone has broken God's law. Because of sin, "all the world" has "become guilty before God. Therefore by the deeds of the law there shall no flesh be justified in his sight: for by the law is the knowledge of sin" (Romans 3:19, 20). But there is hope in Jesus. "The promise by faith of Jesus Christ" is "given to them that believe" (Galatians 3:22).

The law is not opposed to the gospel, because the law does not attempt to do what Jesus alone can do. Nor should we ever try to make the law do what it cannot do. But the law is to be obeyed by Jesus' power in the life of the believer. This is Paul's point in the epistles to the Romans and the Galatians.

Before Faith Came

"Before faith came, we were kept under the law, shut up unto the faith which should afterwards be revealed. Wherefore the law was our schoolmaster to bring us unto Christ, that we might be justified by faith. But after that faith is come, we are no longer under a schoolmaster" (Galatians 3:23-25).

"Before faith came" in the context of the passage means before the cross. Notice the context:

Verse 17: The law was given 430 years after the covenant promises were made to Abraham.

Verse 19: The law "was added because of transgressions, *till the seed should come.*"

Verse 24. "So that the law was our custodian *until Christ came*" (RSV).

Verse 25: "After that faith is come," that is, after the coming of Christ, "we are no longer under a schoolmaster."

Galatians 4:1-5 clinches the point by likening Israel before the cross to a wealthy man's child, treated in some respects like a slave under "guardians and trustees" (RSV), until his father chooses to give him his inheritance. The point at which Israel ceased to be under guardians and trustees and received the promised inheritance was the coming of Christ. "When the fulness of the time was come, God sent forth his Son, made of a woman, made under the law, to redeem them that were under the law, that we might receive the adoption of sons" (Galatians 4:4, 5). Therefore the sentence, "before faith came, we were confined under the law" (Galatians 3:23, RSV) means that before the cross, Israelites and the world in general were under the law in some sense in which they are no longer under the law after the cross. The law functioned like a "schoolmaster" (KJV) or "custodian" (RSV) until Christ came, at which time we ceased to be "under a schoolmaster" (verses 24, 25). So, in a sense, faith and justification, freedom from "tutors and governors" (KJV), "guardians and trustees" (4:2, RSV) did not occur until "the fulness of the time" when "God sent forth His Son" into the world (compare Galatians 3:24, 25 with 4:1-4).

In our last chapter we quoted Ellen G. White's statement identifying the "schoolmaster" of Galatians 3:24 with "both the ceremonial and the moral code of ten commandments." She wrote of Galatians 3:24: "In this scripture, the Holy Spirit through the apostle is speaking especially of the moral law" (*Selected Messages*, bk. 1, p. 234).

The Greek word translated "schoolmaster" in the King James Version of Galatians 3:24, 25 does not mean a school-teacher. Arndt and Gingrich's *Greek-English Lexicon of the New Testament* gives the meaning of the word: ". . . *attendant (slave), custodian, guide*, literally 'boy-leader', the man, usually a slave . . . whose duty it was to conduct the boy or youth . . . to and from school and to superintend his conduct generally; he was not a 'teacher' (despite the present meaning of the derivative 'pedagogue' . . .)."

Hence, Paul used the custodian of children, whose task was to supervise their conduct and lead them safely to and from school, to illustrate the manner in which the law functioned before the cross. The law had the general oversight of Israel, and, for that matter, of the entire world, guiding conduct and directing people to the Messiah, whose coming would bring them into their legal inheritance, providing the fruition of faith in the form of ultimate forgiveness for sin. "So that the law was our custodian until Christ came, that we might be justified by faith" (Galatians 3:24, RSV).

The problem should now be obvious. Is Paul contradicting what he has said elsewhere about the law continuing to function after the cross as the standard of righteousness? The answer is, No! The legalistic Jewish Christians were exalting law keeping as the means of salvation. Paul contradicted them, asserting that faith (grace) is the only means of salvation. Then he answered the logical question: Why was the law given? He answered that it was given to point out sin, condemn the sinner to death, and lead him to Christ.

But if the law functioned as a custodian before the cross in a manner in which it does not function after the cross; if faith and justification do not come until the cross, are we not forced to admit that the means of salvation before the cross were different from what they are now? Once again the answer is negative. Before the cross, salvation was by faith (grace) alone. This is the major emphasis of the epistle to the Galatians (compare Galatians 3:6-9, 14 with Romans 4 and Hebrews 11). When Paul wrote that "the just shall live by faith" (Romans 1:17; see also Galatians 3:11; Hebrews 10:38), he was quoting the Old Testament. Habakkuk 2:4 says: "The just shall live by his faith." The message of the book of Deuteronomy, which Paul appropriated, is that salvation is only by faith (compare Deuteronomy 6:4-6; 10:16; 30:6, 11-14 with Romans 2:25-29; 10:6-10).

Was Old Testament mankind "under the law" (Galatians 3:23) in a different sense than we are today? Three important points must be made in answer to this question:

1. Legal justification could not be given until Christ died for the sins of the world. The sins of Old Testament believers were forgiven when they confessed by virtue of the merits of the coming Messiah. Abraham was justified by faith (see Genesis 15:6; Romans 4:3; Galatians 3:6). So were all Old Testament believers. But the forgiveness (justification) granted to Old Testament believers depended on Christ's suffering the punishment for their guilt. "A death has occurred which redeems them from the transgressions under the first covenant" (Hebrews 9:15, RSV). Forgiveness (justification) before the cross was conditional upon Christ's successfully atoning for human sin.

Writing of the resurrection, Paul emphasized the point: "If

Christ be not raised, your faith is vain; ye are yet in your sins. Then they also which are fallen asleep in Christ are perished" (1 Corinthians 15:17, 18). The significance of that passage is enormous! Abraham and a host of believers before the cross fell asleep in Christ. But if Christ had not succeeded in His mission, if He had not risen from the dead, no Old Testament believer would ever be raised from the grave.

Old Testament believers were conditionally forgiven for sin. From a legal point of view, the law imprisoned mankind before the cross under condemnation to eternal death until the penalty for sin was paid by Jesus Christ. The cross brought a dramatic change for all humanity. Faith reached its fulfillment when Jesus died and rose again. Justification finally became a legal reality, not only for the worthies who died in hope before the cross but also for all those Christians who look back to Christ's sacrifice and forward to the eternal kingdom.

Before the cross the law was doing its appointed task of condemning the whole world to eternal death. Those who were conditionally forgiven before the cross have now received legal justification. Because the sacrifice for sin has been paid, the only condition for justification now is that we accept Jesus as our Saviour (see Romans 5:16-21). This simply means that justification received by faith in Christ results in eternal life. But it must be received! *"They which receive abundance of grace and of the gift of righteousness shall reign in life by one, Jesus Christ"* (Romans 5:17, italics supplied).

2. Before the cross the law was God's appointed agency for revealing human sin. From the fall of our first parents the moral law revealed human sin. The Ten Commandments were spoken and written at Sinai as a special means of awakening Israelites and the world in general to the terrible nature of evil (see Galatians 3:19; Romans 5:20). The ceremonial law dramatized the dire results of sin by daily demonstrating the suffering that would be endured by the coming Messiah.

"When the fullness of the time was come" (Galatians 4:4), Jesus brought a change. He did not abolish any of the Ten Commandments (see Matthew 5:17-20), but He gave the world a demonstration of how they should be kept. His life was a perfect example of the principles of His own law. Christ surpasses the law as a revealer of human sin; His perfect life more effectively exposes sin than does the law (see 1 Peter 2:21, 22; Philippians 2:5). When we see the contrast between our sin and Jesus' holiness, we crave to be overcomers and be like Him. Although the law still functions as a mirror of human sin (see James 1:22-25), when Jesus came the law ceased to be the *primary* means by which our weakness and need are revealed to us.

3. The law (moral and ceremonial) provided the primary revelation of God to Old Testament mankind. The teachings of the prophets were designed to bring Israel back to a relationship with God and so to obedience to His law. At the cross the ceremonial law was replaced by the reality of Christ's death and heavenly ministry (see Hebrews 7-10). The moral law, which so effectively reveals the principles of the government of God, was *not* replaced. But it was surpassed by Christ's supreme demonstration of the infinite love of God. The life and death of Jesus gave humanity the greatest possible revelation of the character of God. To know Christ is to know God (see John 14:9, 10; Hebrews 1:3).

Galatians 3:23-25 certainly relates to our experience today. Before we had faith in Christ we were "confined under the law" (verse 23, RSV). We were no better off than the people before Christ's death. In fact, we were in a much worse condition than Old Testament believers. At least they had the hope that the Messiah was coming. We had no hope. Christ had died for our sin, but we had not accepted Him. We were under condemnation to eternal death (see Romans 6:23), the victim of our fallen humanity (see Romans 8:5, 7, 8), alienated from God (see Ephesians 2:1-3), with no hope of life beyond the grave. What greater bondage could there be than that? Only when we found Christ were we released from this imprisonment in sin (see Ephesians 2:4-6). The law did what it was intended to do; it condemned us to death. Then we found Christ, and His law became our delight (see Romans 7:12, 14; 8:3, 4).

Summary

The law before the cross was a "custodian," condemning all humanity to death until the penalty for sin was paid. It also revealed the perfection of God's character and, by contrast, the ugliness of sin. Because of Christ's death, ultimate justification has been made available to both Old and New Testament mankind. Since Christ's coming, although the moral law continues to reveal God's character and to expose human sin, Christ fulfills these functions more effectively. We have now received the inheritance spoken of in Galatians 4:1-5: redemption from sin and adoption as sons and daughters of God.

Chapter 9
Released Slaves

Galatians 3:26—4:20

At times during His earthly ministry Jesus rested from the constant pressure of teaching and healing to revitalize His spiritual and physical resources. On one such occasion, craving a degree of solitude, He "withdrew to the district of Tyre and Sidon" (Matthew 15:21, RSV). Yet He was not thinking only of His personal needs. His disciples had not yet caught a vision of God's love for the Gentile world. In conformity with attitudes generally adopted by their own people, the disciples imagined that, because they were the favored race, all others were excluded from the spiritual advantages bestowed upon them. Jesus wanted to expose them to an experience that would dispel that illusion and awaken in their hearts love and sympathy for all humanity.

"Behold, a Canaanite woman from that region came out and cried, 'Have mercy on me, O Lord, Son of David; my daughter is severely possessed by a demon'" (Matthew 15:22, RSV). Initially Jesus acted in a manner that the disciples thought thoroughly appropriate. He ignored the woman. After all, the disciples thought, as a heathen she could not expect the Lord to respond to her plea. By racial heritage she was excluded from the advantages enjoyed by the Jews.

Jesus was not able or even willing to hide His loving concern for the poor woman, who demonstrated that she had hope and faith enough to persist with her plea. The disciples "begged him, saying, 'Send her away, for she is crying

91

after us'" (Matthew 15:23, RSV). With sorrow and pity in His heart, yet still anxious to give the disciples a picture of their own selfish chauvinism, Jesus answered, "'I was sent only to the lost sheep of the house of Israel'" (verse 24, RSV).

The woman was not turned away. She had heard of Jesus' ministry of mercy, she detected the concern that He could not hide, and she pressed her petition more insistently: "'Lord, help me'" (Matthew 15:25, RSV). Jesus expressed the unspoken response of His disciples: "'It is not fair to take the children's bread and throw it to the dogs'" (Matthew 15:26, RSV). Heathen Gentiles were dogs in the estimation of some who claimed to be children of God.

The woman's faith rose to the occasion. "'Yes, Lord, yet even the dogs eat the crumbs that fall from their masters' table'" (Matthew 15:27, RSV). If only she could be heard and answered, this courageous, faithful woman was happy to be regarded as a dog. Jesus could conceal His love no longer. He answered, "'O woman, great is your faith! Be it done for you as you desire.' And her daughter was healed instantly" (Matthew 15:28, RSV).

"The Saviour is satisfied. He has tested her faith in Him. By His dealings with her, He has shown that she who has been regarded as an outcast from Israel is no longer an alien, but a child in God's household. As a child it is her privilege to share in the Father's gifts. Christ now grants her request, and finishes the lesson to the disciples. . . ."

"The same agencies that barred men away from Christ eighteen hundred years ago are at work today. The spirit which built up the partition wall between Jew and Gentile is still active. Pride and prejudice have built strong walls of separation between different classes of men. Christ and His mission have been misrepresented, and multitudes feel that they are virtually shut away from the ministry of the gospel. But let them not feel that they are shut away from Christ. There are no barriers which man or Satan can erect but that faith can penetrate. . . .

"The blessings of salvation are for every soul. Nothing but his own choice can prevent any man from becoming a partaker of the promise in Christ by the gospel.

"Caste is hateful to God. He ignores everything of this character. In His sight the souls of all men are of equal value. . . . Without distinction of age, or rank, or nationality, or religious privilege, all are invited to come unto Him and live." (*The Desire of Ages*, pp. 401-403).

This same message was reiterated by the apostle Paul in the section of his epistle to the Galatians that we are considering in this chapter (see Galatians 3:26—4:20).

All One in Christ Jesus

Because Christ died for the sins of the whole world, we are no longer under the tutelage of the "schoolmaster" or "custodian," as were people before the cross, and we "all are the children of God by faith in Christ Jesus" (Galatians 3:26). The faithful before the cross were children of God, too, but they had not yet received their inheritance. The death of Christ changed the picture. Justification, without the condition that a sacrifice for sin needed to be offered, became available to all humanity because the penalty for sin was now paid. "As one man's trespass led to condemnation for all men, so one man's act of righteousness leads to acquittal and life for all men" (Romans 5:18, RSV). That means "all men" who are willing to receive the justification that Christ has earned for them. The preceding verse reads: "If, because of one man's trespass, death reigned through that one man, much more will *those who receive* the abundance of grace and the free gift of righteousness reign in life through the one man Jesus Christ" (Romans 5:17, RSV, italics supplied; compare Galatians 3:29).

"As many of you as were baptized into Christ have put on Christ" (Galatians 3:27, RSV). What does it mean to "put on Christ"? Paul spoke of "Christ in you, the hope of glory" (Colossians 1:27). He identified the presence of Christ as the Holy Spirit in the heart of the believer (see Romans 8:9, 10; Ephesians 3:16, 17). Paul underlined the teaching of Jesus that the believer receives the baptism of the Holy Spirit in the new-birth experience (see John 3:5-7). Water baptism follows as the evidence of the transformation that has already taken place. To be a child of God who has received the gift of eternal life without any legal conditions, because the sacrifice for sin has been offered, we must all accept by faith the presence of the Holy Spirit into our hearts. Jesus promised: "I will pray the Father, and he shall give you another Comforter, that he may abide with you for ever; even the Spirit of truth; . . . for he dwelleth with you, and shall be in you. I will not leave you comfortless: I will come to you" (John 14:16-18).

Spiritual unity is inevitable among those who have received Christ into their hearts by the Holy Spirit. Paul wrote of the bond of love and fellowship made possible by the cross: "There is neither Jew nor Greek, there is neither slave nor free, there is neither male nor famale; for you are all one in Christ Jesus" (Galatians 3:28, RSV).

The same Holy Spirit who tells you that you are a child of God (see Romans 8:16) impresses you that another person who has accepted Jesus is also a child of God. There is a bond between fellow believers that goes beyond mere common interests and cultural similarities. It is a spiritual bond created by the presence of the Holy Spirit in the hearts of brethren and sisters in Christ.

The Holy Spirit produces holiness of life in people individually and corporately (see Hebrews 2:11). There is a unity of attitude and outlook manifested by those who are in Christ. They love the same basic values and despise evil. They feel comfortable with one another because their reactions, feelings, motives, and ideals are similar (see Luke 8:21).

There is no exaltation of one above another among those who are in Christ, because they accept His example of love and respect for others (see Matthew 20:25, 26; 23:8). Those who are "one in Christ Jesus" (Galatians 3:28) have no desire to gain predominance over others because of racial considerations. The fact that in Christ "there is neither Jew nor Greek" is the basis of their love and acceptance of all races. "There is no difference between Jew and Gentile—the same Lord is Lord of all and richly blesses all who call on him" (Romans 10:12, NIV).

Paul was not attempting to abolish all distinctions of sex,

nationality, race, or social standing. His concern, reflecting that of Jesus, was to stress that salvation is given in the same manner and to the same degree to every believer irrespective of sex, race, or social standing. Our mission as Christians is not to involve ourselves in the political and social movements designed to produce a classless society. Our mission is to convince all classes that, in terms of the gift of Christ's saving grace, they have equal opportunity. There are some distinctions in this imperfect world that we cannot change. But the gospel brings all races and classes of humanity into a bond of love, fellowship, and unity that no human social program can ever hope to duplicate.

Children and Slaves Set Free

Galatians 4:1-7 contrasts the relationship between God and His people before the cross with the relationship since the cross. Because in Old Testament times the penalty for sin had not yet been paid, those who were living by faith in the Messiah to come were like children who are heirs to a vast estate but who cannot receive their inheritance until a specified time in the future. Believers before the cross were under "tutors and governors" until the coming of the Messiah (see Galatians 4:2). The "tutors and governors" (KJV) or "guardians and trustees" (RSV) refer to the law of God (compare Galatians 3:24, 25).

Just as a child who is an heir to a fortune will often be directed and controlled by a guardian until he or she comes of age, so believers before the cross were guided and instructed by the moral and ceremonial laws. Once Christ had died, justification in an ultimate legal sense was made available to all humanity, and the moral law ceased to condemn believers before and after the cross. As explained in the previous chapter, even though Old Testament believers were forgiven for their sins (justified), their eternal salvation was not sealed until Christ bore their punishment on the cross. At the same point the ceremonial law was replaced by the reality of Christ's sacrifice and heavenly High Priest ministry.

"When the time had fully come, God sent forth his Son,

born of woman, born under the law, to redeem those who were under the law, so that we might receive adoption as sons" (Galatians 4:4, 5, RSV). Now we are no longer under "the elemental spirits of the universe" (Galatians 4:3, RSV). The law no longer condemns believers; the law is no longer the supreme revelation of God's character; nor is the law the supreme means by which God shows us our sin. The law remains as the divine standard of righteousness (see Romans 3:31; 7:7; 8:3, 4). But Jesus' perfect life surpasses the law as a revelation of God's character and as the means by which our sins are pointed out to us. Jesus is now our guardian and trustee. We are sons and daughters of God who have entered into our inheritance. Because Christ has died and we have received Him by faith, eternal life has begun for us (see 1 John 5:11-13). "Wherefore thou art no more a servant, but a son; and if a son, then an heir of God through Christ" (Galatians 4:7).

From One False Religion to Another

Paul explained to the Galatian Christians that, by accepting the teachings of the Judaizers, they were substituting their old heathen religion for an equally barren system (see Galatians 4:8-10). The gods they served before they accepted Christ were nonexistent. They were then in bondage to superstition and error. Because they were now turning to the law as the means of salvation, they were exposing themselves to the same alienation from God as they had suffered before.

Paul had already explained that the law had a correct function before the cross (see Galatians 3:19—4:7). But its function was never to make the sinner righteous or to give him salvation. Paul was saying, "The cross brought a change in the relationship of believers to the law. But never at any stage, before or after the cross, was lawkeeping to be the means by which humanity was to be saved from sin. Law points out sin and directs the believer to Christ as the only Saviour. If you turn to the law as the means of salvation, you are as lost as any heathen serving nonexistent gods."

The "days, and months, and seasons, and years" (Galatians

4:10, RSV) refer to the occasions on which special ceremonial animal sacrifices were offered at the temple (see Leviticus 23; Numbers 28). Paul was not depreciating the seventh-day Sabbath as a memorial of Creation. The weekly Sabbath was instituted by the Creator Himself at the end of creation week (see Genesis 2:1-3; compare Exodus 20:8-11). Jesus instructed His followers to observe the Sabbath until the end of human history (see Matthew 24:20). Paul himself faithfully observed the weekly Sabbath (see Acts 13, 16-18).

The Galatians had accepted the demand of the legalistic Jewish Christians that they should observe the ceremonial law.

Paul's Appeal

Paul was not content only to answer the arguments of the Judaizers and to explain true doctrine to the Galatian Christians. He spoke to their hearts. He had given up legalistic Judaism and had devoted his life to tireless ministry to the Gentiles. Why should the Galatian Christians turn to the legalistic system from which Paul had been delivered (see Galatians 4:12)? He earnestly endeavored to lead them again into the experience of righteousness and salvation by faith in Christ.

The Galatian Christians had loved Paul. They had ministered to his physical needs and had received him as if he were an angel from heaven (see Galatians 4:13, 14). Paul pleaded with them: "What has become of the satisfaction you felt? . . . Have I then become your enemy by telling you the truth?" (Galatians 4:15, 16, RSV). It was inconceivable to Paul that their love and dedication could so soon be turned to resentment toward himself and alienation from Christ.

The real culprits were the legalists who had deceived the Galatian Christians (see Galatians 4:17, 18). Their motives were open to question. Paul saw them as self-serving. Their real intent was not to teach truth, but to exalt themselves by winning the loyalty of the Galatians to their religious beliefs and practices. How like some members of the church today! They seek recognition by insisting that they have truth superior to that of their brethren and sisters. If only everyone would follow their particular ideas, all could have salvation.

"While they trust to the guidance of human authority, none will come to a saving knowledge of the truth. Like Nathanael, we need to study God's word for ourselves, and pray for the enlightenment of the Holy Spirit. He who saw Nathanael under the fig tree will see us in the secret place of prayer. Angels from the world of light are near to those who in humility seek for divine guidance" (*The Desire of Ages*, p. 141).

Our great need, like that of the Galatian Christians, is that "Christ be formed" in us (Galatians 4:19). When the Holy Spirit is received into our hearts by faith, Christ is formed in us. "Christ alone can help us and give us the victory. Christ must be all in all to us, He must dwell in the heart, His life must circulate through us as the blood circulates through the veins. His Spirit must be a vitalizing power that will cause us to influence others to become Christlike and holy" (*SDA Bible Commentary*, vol. 5, p. 1144).

Summary

Since the cross, believers are sons and daughters of God who have entered into their inheritance. Salvation is by faith in Christ irrespective of race, social standing, or sex. As by faith we receive Christ into our hearts, we have freedom from the bondage of legalism and sin.

Chapter 10
Two Ways for Travelers

Galatians 4:21-31

When we were living in Angwin, California, there were two ways we could take if we wanted to drive to St. Helena. We could turn right from the driveway of our yard and travel over the hill near our home, or we could turn left and travel around the hill. Because both ways were acceptable—we sometimes took one and sometimes took the other.

Although the Bible presents two ways that have been taken by travelers setting out for the heavenly kingdom, there is only one that will lead to that destination. In his epistles, Paul pleads with his readers to reject the false way and to remain faithful to the true way. The false way is the "old covenant," and the true way is the "new covenant." Paradoxically, the new covenant is older than the old covenant. The new covenant is the plan for the redemption of mankind that God devised in the eternal ages before the creation of our world. It is called the new covenant because it involves a brand new experience with Christ for every believer who turns to Him for salvation.

The Formation of the New Covenant

In the eternal ages before He created our world, God decided how He would save humanity if they chose to sin. Because God could see into the future, He knew that humans would choose to sin. The new covenant was the plan He worked out to save those who would be sorry for their sins and would turn to Him for deliverance.

Paul wrote of "eternal life, which God, that cannot lie, promised before the world began" (Titus 1:2). He taught that God "hath saved us, and called us with an holy calling, not according to our works, but according to his own purpose and grace, which was given us in Christ Jesus before the world began" (2 Timothy 1:9). There are two ways for travelers: (1) "our works" and (2) "his own purpose and grace." God knew that no sinner would be able to atone for his sin by his own works. He planned that every sinner who would believe in the sacrifice of Christ would be given righteousness and salvation by grace.

"The terms of this oneness between God and man in the great covenant of redemption were arranged with Christ from all eternity. . . . The covenant of grace is not a new truth, for it existed in the mind of God from all eternity. This is why it is called the everlasting covenant. The plan of redemption was not conceived after the fall of man to cure the dreadful evil; the apostle Paul speaks of the gospel, the preaching of Jesus Christ, as 'the revelation of the mystery which hath been kept in silence through times eternal, but now is manifested' " (Ellen G. White, *The Signs of the Times*, August 24, 1891).

The Covenant Revealed After the Fall

As soon as Adam and Eve sinned they were offered the everlasting covenant relationship with God as the means by which they could be saved. The promise of the Messiah contained in Genesis 3:15 meant that, if Adam and Eve believed in His sacrifice for them, they would be given His righteousness and, ultimately, the privilege of living for eternity. "I will put enmity between thee [Satan] and the woman [the church], and between thy seed [Satan's followers] and her seed [believers in Christ]; it shall bruise thy [Satan's] head, and thou shalt bruise his [Christ's] heel" (Genesis 3:15). The Messiah (Christ) would suffer for human sin, but would rise from the dead. He would defeat Satan, who finally would be destroyed for eternity.

"The covenant of grace was first made with man in Eden, when after the Fall there was given a divine promise that the seed of the woman should bruise the serpent's head. To all men this covenant offered pardon and the assisting grace of God for future obedience through faith in Christ. It also promised them eternal life on condition of fidelity to God's law. Thus the patriarchs received the hope of salvation" (*Patriarchs and Prophets*, p. 370).

After their fall into sin, our first parents and their children were commanded to offer animal sacrifices to remind them that the Messiah was coming to die for them. The offering of these sacrifices was to be an act of faith, and it was also to be the means by which their faith could be kept strong. "By faith Abel offered unto God a more excellent sacrifice than Cain, by which he obtained witness that he was righteous, God testifying of his gifts" (Hebrews 11:4). Abel was living under the everlasting covenant of righteousness by faith. But Cain was living under the old covenant of works. Instead of demonstrating faith in the Messiah to come by offering animal sacrifices, Cain presented to the Lord the produce of the ground, the result of his own labor (see Genesis 4:3-5). The first murder was committed by one who had rejected God's way and had chosen to seek favor by his own works.

All the patriarchs who followed Adam and Abel were offered salvation by faith in the Messiah to come. They did their best to convince the wicked people of their own time that God's way was the only way. Noah is a typical example. He "became heir of the righteousness which is by faith" (Hebrews 11:7). After the Flood, Noah was told that the rainbow in the clouds would be God's sign to the faithful that His everlasting covenant would never depart from them (see Isaiah 54:9, 10).

"The rainbow spanning the heavens with its arch of light is a token of 'the everlasting covenant between God and every living creature.' Genesis 9:16. And the rainbow encircling the throne on high is also a token to God's children of His covenant of peace" (*Education*, p. 115).

The Covenant With Abraham

Because Abraham believed God's promises, the righteousness of Christ was bestowed upon him by the Holy Spirit (see Genesis 15:6; Galatians 3:1-9, 14). The Lord promised Abraham that the Messiah would be one of his descendants (see Genesis 12:3; Galatians 3:8). He promised him that he would be the father of the multitudes of the faithful till the end of time (see Genesis 17:8; Galatians 3:7; Romans 4:11, 12). He promised him that the land of Canaan would be the heritage of his children as a type of the heavenly Canaan that would be theirs for eternity (see Hebrews 11:8-11).

When Abraham entered into a heart relationship with God, he had the power to obey the divine law. The Lord expected this of him (see Genesis 17:1). When the Lord, by the Holy Spirit, comes to dwell in a human heart, He expects that person to live for Him. He expects that person to turn away from sin and do the things His law requires. God was able to say of Abraham: "Abraham obeyed my voice, and kept my charge, my commandments, my statutes, and my laws" (Genesis 26:5).

Abraham had some serious lapses into sin. He did not always live under the everlasting covenant of righteousness by faith. Like Cain, there were times in Abraham's life when he attempted to earn God's promises by his own works. Unlike Cain, Abraham repented before it was too late. The Lord promised Abraham that his son by Sarah would inherit the covenant promises and be the forerunner of the Messiah (see Genesis 15:4). When the fulfillment of the promise was delayed because Sarah was barren, both Abraham and Sarah became impatient. Sarah gave Abraham her maid, Hagar, as a concubine so that they could have a son by her (see Genesis 16:1-16).

In writing to the Galatians, the apostle Paul used Abraham's lapse as evidence of the terrible results of attempting to be saved "under the law" (see Galatians 4:21). Those who try to work their way to heaven, ignorning God's way, are bound to failure. Paul used Hagar and Ishmael as symbols of the old covenant of independent human works (see Galatians 4:22-24).

By contrast, when Abraham trusted God to fulfill His promise of giving him a son by Sarah, despite their advanced age, he was living under the new covenant, the everlasting covenant of righteousness and salvation by faith. (Compare Galatians 4:22-24 with Genesis 17:15-21.) Paul used Sarah and Isaac to represent the new covenant of grace.

The Covenant With Israel at Sinai

Paul identified the Sinai covenant with the old covenant of works symbolized by Hagar and Ishmael. "Hagar is Mount Sinai in Arabia, she corresponds to the present Jerusalem, for she is in slavery with her children" (Galatians 4:25, RSV). Did God offer Israel a different covenant from that offered to Abraham?

The Lord had promised Abraham that the same covenant relationship that he enjoyed with God would be offered to all his descendants. "I will establish my covenant between me and you and *your descendants after you throughout their generations* for an everlasting covenant, to be God to you and to your descendants after you" (Genesis 17:7, RSV, italics supplied; compare verses 9 and 19). We can assume, therefore, that when God offered Abraham's descendants "my covenant," it was the same covenant that He had offered Abraham. God's terms were not always accepted by Abraham's descendants, nor was the resulting relationship between God and His people always according to His will. Even so, it is clear that God's terms were always the same: righteousness and salvation by faith in the Messiah to come.

Centuries after Abraham's death the Lord offered Israel at Sinai "my covenant" (Exodus 19:5). The terms of the covenant were identical to those given to Abraham: The Israelites were to trust God, believing in the Messiah to come, and relying on the Lord for grace to obey His law. The tragedy is that Israel attempted to obey in their own strength. Like Cain they attempted to save themselves instead of relying totally on the Lord. Like Abraham in his marriage to Hagar, they tried to fulfill the promises in their own way. The result was that they lost their vision of the Lord, built the golden calf, and entered into an orgy of idolaltry and immorality. Their promises of obedience were like ropes of sand (see Exodus 19:8; 24:3, 7; Deuteronomy 5:27-29).

The Lord had wanted Israel to have a heart relationship with Himself that no temptation to sin could transcend. Instead, the resulting "covenant" was a perversion of God's terms; Israel substituted the old covenant of works for the covenant of grace (see Jeremiah 31:31-33; Hebrews 8:8-13). This is why Paul identified Israel's Sinai experience with Abraham's marriage to Hagar (see Galatians 4:24, 25).

The terms of the covenant that God *offered* Israel were identical to those offered to Abraham and those offered to us today (see Galatians 3:15-18; Psalm 105:8-11; Jeremiah 11:1-7).

"The covenant that God made with His people at Sinai is to be our refuge and defense. . . .

" 'And Moses came and called for the elders of the people, and laid before their faces all these words.'

" 'And all the people answered together, and said, All that the Lord hath spoken we will do.'

"This covenant is of just as much force today as it was when the Lord made it with ancient Israel" (*SDA Bible Commentary*, vol. 1, p. 1103).

The Jerusalem of Paul's day was "in slavery with her children" (Galatians 4:25) because the Israelites were making the same mistake that Cain and Abraham, and Israel at Sinai had made. They believed that they were acceptable to God because of their law keeping. They had replaced the faith-grace relationship with the Lord, which makes possible genuine obedience to the divine commands by a monstrous system of righteousness by works. Legalism replaced faith, self-righteousness was substituted for Christ's righteousness, and bondage to sin took the place of spiritual freedom in Christ.

The Two Covenants: Two Ministries

Because at Sinai Israel failed to enter into the everlasting covenant relationship with Him, the Lord gave Moses more

detailed instructions regarding animal sacrifices and ceremonies that pointed forward to the sacrifice and ministry of the
Messiah. The details of the ceremonial law, with the ministry of
priests in the earthly sanctuary, were God's way of meeting the
spiritual emergency created by the failure of His people.

Something bad led to something good: the old covenant of
works created by Israel at Sinai resulted in the temporary
ministry of Levitical priests in the services of the sanctuary or
temple. In the epistle to the Hebrews we are told that this
temporary earthly ministry, which met its reality when Christ
died on the cross, was also part of the "old covenant." By contrast, the ministry of Christ is "the surety of a better
covenant" (Hebrews 7:22, RSV). "The first covenant had
regulations for worship and an earthly sanctuary" (Hebrews
9:1, RSV).

The point was not that the sanctuary services were intended by God to be part of a system of works-righteousness,
even though the Jews observed these services in a legalistic
manner. God's intention was that the temporary ceremonial
system would strengthen the faith of His people and
demonstrate that they genuinely believed in the work of the
coming Messiah. But the ceremonial system was temporary.
For the Galatians to revert to its observance was to nullify the
achievements of Calvary.

In the New Testament the old covenant, or first covenant,
consisted of something bad and something good:

1. Something bad: The attempt to earn righteousness by
works; the faulty human response to God's terms (see Galatians 4:21-31).

2. Something good: The temporary sanctuary ministry instituted by God because His people had failed. Through the
ceremonial system the Lord sought to lead His people to salvation by grace (see Hebrews 7:11-28).

Likewise, there are two aspects to the new or everlasting
covenant:

1. The righteousness-by-faith experience, entered into by
those who accept Christ.

2. The sacrifice and heavenly ministry of Christ, by which

His grace is made available to all who believe.

In his epistle to the Galatians, as elsewhere in his writings, Paul repudiated both aspects of the old covenant and pled with the people to enter fully into an everlasting covenant relationship with Christ.

Freedom in Christ

Paul reminded the Galatians that "like Isaac" we "are children of promise" (Galatians 4:28, RSV). As Ishmael persecuted Isaac, so today those who choose to live under the slavery of legalistic religion endeavor to discredit the faithful children of God (see Galatians 4:29). "What does the scripture say? 'Cast out the slave and her son; for the son of the slave shall not inherit with the son of the free woman' " (Galatians 4:30, RSV; compare Genesis 21:1-14).

In Paul's allegory, Hagar and Ishmael represent the old covenant of works-righteousness. As Sarah, with the Lord's approval, insisted on the separation of Hagar and Ishmael from the camp of Abraham, so we are to have done forever with man-made religion. "We are not children of the slave but of the free woman" (Galatians 4:31, RSV). United with Christ, we are freed from the bondage of legalism, freed from the inevitable spiritual failure involved in the attempt to earn favor with God, freed from the condemnation of the law (see Romans 8:1). In Christ, there is peace (see Romans 5:1), victory over sin (see 1 John 5:4), and joy because of the Holy Spirit's indwelling (see Romans 14:17).

Summary

The two ways for travelers are God's way and Satan's. God's way is for all to enter into the everlasting covenant of righteousness and salvation by faith. Satan's counterfeit, the old covenant, invites us to substitute our own efforts for Christ's grace. The Lord's appeal, so eloquently expressed by the apostle Paul, is that we enter into a heart relationship with Him, depending solely upon Him, abiding in Him, and enjoying perpetually the fruits of righteousness.

Chapter 11
The Continuing Battle for Freedom

Galatians 5:1-15

A friend once told the philosopher-poet Samuel Taylor Coleridge that he did not believe that children should be given any religious instruction. He argued that a child's mind should not be biased in any direction; he should be permitted to choose his own religious faith when he had developed sufficient maturity.

Coleridge remained silent. He asked the friend whether he would care to see his garden. The man said he would, and Coleridge took him to the back of the house and out into the garden. The man was shocked by what he saw. He said, "This is not a garden. You are growing nothing but weeds."

Coleridge replied, "Well, you see I did not wish to infringe upon the liberty of the garden in any way. I was just giving the garden a chance to express itself and to choose its own production."

The philosophy of education that leaves a child's mind to the devil is totally contrary to the instruction given in the Word of God. "Train up a child in the way he should go: and when he is old, he will not depart from it" (Proverbs 22:6). "These words, which I command thee this day, shall be in thine heart: and thou shalt teach them diligently unto thy children, and shalt talk of them when thou sittest in thine house, and when thou walkest by the way, and when thou liest down, and when thou risest up" (Deuteronomy 6:6, 7).

Adult minds, like those of children, are not to be left fallow so that any and every erroneous philosophy might take root. Christian freedom is not freedom from truth, from righteousness, from obedience to God's laws, and from commitment to an ordered manner of life.

Some Christians imagine that justification is like an umbrella over them, ensuring their salvation despite the sins in their lives. "Some will not make a right use of the doctrine of justification by faith. They will present it in a one-sided manner. Others will seize the ideas that have not been correctly presented, and will go clear over the mark, ignoring works altogether" (*Selected Messages*, bk. 2, p. 20).

Herein lies one of the major problems among Christians today. Justification is depicted as only a legal declaration in heaven involving the righteousness of Christ being placed to the believer's account. That declaration remains legally valid, so we are told, whatever the sins of the believer. Works of any kind are regarded as irrelevant to salvation. Christian standards of behavior are thought of as legalism. The Christian who is under Christ's grace is said to be free from the stipulations of the law. Freedom is defined as legal justification which cannot be abrogated by sin in the life; only outright rejection of Christ can change the picture, they claim.

If this doctrine were true, Christ's sacrifice would save us *in* our sins, not "*from* our sins" (see Matthew 1:21). If this doctrine were true, Paul should never have spoken of justified believers as "slaves of righteousness" (Romans 6:18, RSV). He never should have rejoiced that Christ died, "in order that the just requirement of the law might be fulfilled in us, who walk not according to the flesh but according to the Spirit" (Romans 8:4, RSV). He never should have identified justification with the gift of the Holy Spirit to the believer's heart (see Galatians 3:1-3, 14; Romans 8:9, 10). In effect, these people are saying that Paul should have argued that the believer is still counted holy, whatever the sins in his or her life.

"The apostle says, 'With the heart man believeth unto righteousness' (Romans 10:10). No one can believe with the heart unto righteousness, and obtain justification by faith, while continuing the practice of those things which the Word of God forbids, or while neglecting any known duty.

"Genuine faith will be manifested in good works; for good works are the fruits of faith. As God works in the heart, and man surrenders his will to God, and cooperates with God, he works out in the life what God works in by the Holy Spirit, and there is harmony between the purpose of the heart and the practice of the life. Every sin must be renounced as the hateful thing that crucified the Lord of life and glory, and the believer must have a progressive experience by continually doing the works of Christ. *It is by continual surrender of the will, by continual obedience, that the blessing of justification is retained*" (*Selected Messages*, bk. 1, pp. 396, 397, italics supplied).

In the first four chapters of his epistle to the Galatians, Paul presents the true doctrine of justification and the correct function of the law before and after the cross. In chapters 5 and 6 he outlines the results in the life. Galatians 5:1-15 deals with freedom in Christ.

The Threat to Freedom in Christ

"It is for freedom that Christ has set us free. Stand firm, then, and do not let yourselves be burdened again by a yoke of slavery" (Galatians 5:1, NIV). What is the "yoke of slavery" that destroys freedom in Christ? Paul gives two answers: (1) the continued observance of the ceremonial law; (2) attempting to be justified by law keeping.

"Now I, Paul, say to you that if you receive circumcision, Christ will be of no advantage to you" (Galatians 5:2, RSV). Paul does not object to circumcision as a means of ensuring physical health. He objects to circumcision as a religious rite that is supposed to bring a man into a right relationship with God. It so happened that the immediate problem in Galatia centered on the question of circumcision. The deeper issue was the attitude by which the Galatians had become convinced that obedience to law was the *means* of salvation.

Because circumcision, along with every other ceremonial

law, pointed forward to the saving work of Jesus Christ, it lost its significance at the cross. Outward circumcision was intended to symbolize the circumcision of the heart made possible by the work of the Messiah (see Deuteronomy 10:16; 30:6; Romans 2:25-29). The point is that the continued practice of circumcision as a religious rite after the cross nullified the significance of Christ's sacrifice.

"I testify again to every man who receives circumcision that he is bound to keep the whole law. You are severed from Christ, you who would be justified by the law; you have fallen away from grace. For through the Spirit, by faith, we wait for the hope of righteousness" (Galatians 5:3-5, RSV). Modern antinomians, who think the Ten Commandments were done away at the cross, seize onto this passage as evidence that those who accept Christ and do not practice circumcision as a religious rite do not have to keep the law. After all, they argue, if the practice of circumcision logically required conformity to the "whole law," rejection of circumcision logically implies conformity to no law.

They fail to understand Paul's point. He was saying, "If you think that you are justified by the practice of circumcision, you must realize that justification by law keeping requires perfect obedience to every law of God. The only person who is right with God by obedience to law is the one who has never broken the law. Because we have broken it, we can be saved only by grace. But this grace does not release us from obedience to God's law. 'For in Christ Jesus neither circumcision nor uncircumcision is of any avail, *but faith working through love*'" (Galatians 5:6, RSV; compare James 2:14-17).

We are justified by faith in Christ. Faith does not earn justification. Our faith is called forth by God's grace, and we receive His saving grace when we have faith.

What is the result? We work through love. What kind of works do we perform? "Do we then overthrow the law by this faith? By no means! On the contrary, we uphold the law" (Romans 3:31, RSV). The law is upheld in our lives when we have faith, because we now have the presence of Christ in our hearts by the Holy Spirit as the power to obey His law. In fact,

His divine presence is the means by which the law of God is written on our hearts (see Romans 10:8-10). Paul opposes "works of the law" (Romans 3:20, RSV) by which a person attempts to earn acceptance with God by law keeping. But, like James, he extols works of faith, by which the justified believer obeys God's law (compare Romans 2:13; James 1:22-25; 2:14-17).

"Through the Spirit, by faith, we wait for the hope of righteousness" (Galatians 5:5, RSV). In the preceding verse, Paul is talking about justification. "You who would be justified by the law; you have fallen away from grace" (Galatians 5:4, RSV). How, then, are we justified? We are justified "through the Spirit, by faith" (Galatians 5:5, RSV). The Spirit brings to our hearts the righteousness of Christ (see Galatians 3:1-3, 14; Romans 5:5; 8:9, 10). Justification "through the Spirit, by faith" is not only a legal matter; it involves transformation of heart in the new-birth experience (compare Titus 3:5-7).

Having received this wonderful experience, "we wait for the hope of righteousness" (Galatians 5:5, RSV). We do not have to wait for the gift of righteousness (compare 1 John 2:29; 3:7). When God justifies us, we immediately receive the gift of righteousness as the Holy Spirit comes into our hearts. The hope of righteousness is the "blessed hope, the appearing of the glory of our great God and Savior Jesus Christ, who gave himself for us to redeem us from all iniquity and to purify for himself a people of his own who are zealous for good deeds" (Titus 2:13, 14, RSV).

The good deeds begin as soon we are justified, because we then have the gift of righteousness by the presence of the Holy Spirit. Justification is redemption from iniquity; it is purification of heart as the qualification for heaven. The final consummation of our hope is realized at Christ's second coming when we are taken with Him to the heavenly kingdom (see John 14:1-4; 1 Thessalonians 4:16-18).

The Destructive Effects of Error

The teaching accepted by the Galatians came, not from God, but from the Jewish legalists who had rejected the decisions of the Jerusalem Council (see Galatians 5:7, 8). "A little leaven leavens the whole lump" (verse 9).

The statement is loaded with meaning. A little error cherished by a church member will very likely spread to his family and to the church. The result is confusion, controversy, discouragement, and apostasy.

"One accepts some new and original idea which does not seem to conflict with the truth. He talks of it and dwells upon it until it seems to him to be clothed with beauty and importance, for Satan has power to give this false appearance. At last it becomes the all-absorbing theme, the one great point around which everything centers; and the truth is uprooted from the heart. . . .

"Brethren, as an ambassador of Christ I warn you to beware of these side issues, whose tendency is to divert the mind from the truth. Error is never harmless. It never sanctifies, but always brings confusion and dissension. It is always dangerous. The enemy has great power over minds that are not thoroughly fortified by prayer and established in Bible truth" (*Testimonies*, vol. 5, p. 292).

Paul was confident that the Galatian Christians would see their error and accept his inspired counsel (see Galatians 5:10). The legalists who had led them astray would have to face the judgment of God. They had evidently gone so far as to represent Paul as in support of their views (see verse 11). But Paul was quick to dissociate himself from them. He wrote, "I wish those who unsettle you would mutilate themselves!" (Galatians 5:12, RSV). The New International Version translates the text: "As for those agitators, I wish they would go the whole way and emasculate themselves!"

"In view of the fact that the basic meaning of the verb which Paul uses in expressing his wish is *to cut off*, there are those who think that the apostle voices his desire that the opponents may be 'cut off' from the church. . . . A more reasonable interpretation, however, one which (because it agrees with the use of the verb in such contexts in contemporary sources) is supported by most commentators both ancient and modern, interprets the meaning to be this, that the

THE CONTINUING BATTLE FOR FREEDOM 113

apostle is saying, 'As for these agitators, they had better go the whole way and make eunuchs of themselves!' (N.E.B.). Paul reasons, as it were, as follows: Since circumcision has lost its religious value, it is nothing more than a concision (cf. Philippians 3:2), which differs only in degree but not essentially from the practices of pagan priests, practices well-known to the Galatians. But since the Judaizers who are upsetting the Galatians believe *a little* physical mutilation is of spiritual value, let them be consistent and cut away *more radically*. Let them go all the way, and castrate themselves, thus making eunuchs of themselves like the priests of Cybele in their wild 'devotions.' " (William Hendriksen, *New Testament Commentary, Galatians and Ephesians* [Grand Rapids, Michigan: Baker, 1979], pp. 205, 206; compare Matthew 18:6; Mark 9:42; Luke 17:2).

Freedom to Obey God's Law

"You were called to freedom, brethren; only do not use your freedom as an opportunity for the flesh, but through love be servants of one another" (Galatians 5:13, RSV). The "flesh" in the writings of Paul refers to the sinful practices of those who are unjustified. By contrast, the "Spirit" has reference to the life of obedience to God's law enjoyed by those justified believers who have true freedom in Christ. Freedom is not license to sin; it is the power not to sin. "Let not sin therefore reign in your mortal bodies, to make you obey their passions. Do not yield your members to sin as instruments of wickedness, but yield yourselves to God as men who have been brought from death to life, and your members to God as instruments of righteousness. For sin will have no dominion over you, since you are not under law but under grace" (Romans 6:12-14, RSV).

"The whole law is fulfilled in one word, 'You shall love your neighbor as yourself' " (Galatians 5:14, RSV). In the immediate context, Paul is speaking of the law that controls our relationship with other human beings. Love to one's neighbor summarizes the six commandments that comprise the second half of the Decalogue. However, a person who does not love

God or keep the first half of the Decalogue will never love his neighbor and observe the second part of the Decalogue. A person who genuinely loves his neighbor in the manner indicated by Jesus is a genuine servant of God (see Luke 10:25-36). Jesus emphasized that "on these two commandments [love to God and love to one's neighbor] depend all the law and the prophets" (Matthew 22:40, RSV).

God's law and the law of love are not mutually exclusive; we do not repudiate the Ten Commandments by manifesting love to God and to our neighbors. The principles of the Ten Commandments are manifested in our lives when we love God and our neighbors. "Love is the fulfilling of the law" (Romans 13:10, RSV) in the sense that only as God's love reigns in our hearts are we able to keep His law in a manner that is acceptable to Him. People who truly have Christ's love as the ruling principle of their lives do not "bite and devour one another" (Galatians 5:15). Their love for God and humanity is the great force that motivates them to service and sacrifice for the eternal happiness of others.

Summary

Freedom in Christ experienced by justified believers is not liberty to sin with impunity. It is freedom *from* sin through the power of the indwelling Holy Spirit. Justification is the new-birth experience that introduces the penitent believer to the righteousness of Christ and to the hope of eternal life. Freed from the shackles of evil, the believer now has the love and grace to devote himself with abandon to the service of his fellow human beings.

Chapter 12
Life in the Spirit

Galatians 5:16-26

"This I say then, Walk in the Spirit, and ye shall not fulfil the lust of the flesh" (Galatians 5:16). The Galatians began their Christian walk "in the Spirit" (Galatians 3:3). Like Abraham, they received "the promise of the Spirit through faith" (Galatians 3:14). They were justified by "the washing of rebirth and renewal by the Holy Spirit" (Titus 3:5, NIV). Paul urged that they walk daily in the same manner by which their Christian life was begun: "In the Spirit."

What practical steps can we take to ensure that we are walking "in the Spirit" (Galatians 5:16)? How can we retain His divine presence in our hearts amid the challenges, pleasures, and sorrows of daily existence? Surrender to Christ is not a once-in-a-lifetime thing. We must come to Him each day in prayer and Bible study.

In prayer we commit ourselves to Christ again, asking that He will come into our hearts and dwell with us throughout the experiences of the day. We praise Him for taking charge of our lives, confiding in Him regarding our needs and concerns, and pleading for guidance and deliverance from evil.

"Prayer is the opening of the heart to God as to a friend. Not that it is necessary in order to make known to God what we are, but in order to enable us to receive Him. Prayer does not bring God down to us, but brings us up to Him. . . .

". . . prayer is the key in the hand of faith to unlock heaven's storehouse, where are treasured the boundless resources of Omnipotence."

"Keep your wants, your joys, your sorrows, your cares, and your fears before God. You cannot burden Him; you cannot weary Him. He who numbers the hairs of your head is not indifferent to the wants of His children. 'The Lord is very pitiful, and of tender mercy.' James 5:11. His heart of love is touched by our sorrows and even by our utterances of them. Take to Him everything that perplexes the mind. Nothing is too great for Him to bear, for He holds up worlds, He rules over all the affairs of the universe. Nothing that in any way concerns our peace is too small for Him to notice. . . . The relations between God and each soul are as distinct and full as though there were not another soul upon the earth to share His watchcare, not another soul for whom He gave His beloved Son" (*Steps to Christ*, pp. 93, 94, 95, 100).

Daily Bible study is essential for the Christian who wishes to continue to "walk in the Spirit." In Bible study we allow Christ to speak to us. Jesus said that the Holy Spirit is His representative who will teach us His truth (see John 14:26). When we engage in prayerful Bible study we give Jesus an opportunity to teach us, by the Holy Spirit, the truths of His Word that are especially relevant to our needs.

Having spent time with the Lord by prayer and Bible study, we can expect to have His guidance through our daily activities. Often throughout the day we can speak to Him silently as we engage in our many and varied duties. Christ promised that He will be with us always (see Matthew 28:20).

When we are tempted at various times through the day, we can confidently pray three prayers: (1) "Lord, I am helpless; I like this sin and will fall without Your power." (2) "Lord, give me the grace not to commit this sin." (3) "Thank You, Lord; I believe You have answered my prayer." Do not forget the third prayer. Faith is praise! Praise Him for giving you the victory, even before you realize the answer to your prayer. It is always God's will to give us power over sin. The Holy Spirit gives you the strength not to sin, and He is constantly imparting the grace to remain gentle and kind as Jesus is.

Life "in the Spirit" is not complete unless we are sharing with others the blessings the Lord has imparted to us. To store His blessings in our hearts as though they are a secret is to lose them ourselves. "The Spirit and the bride say, Come" (Revelation 22:17). As believers in Christ, we are part of His "bride," the church (Revelation 19:7, 8), which has the responsibility of extending His loving invitations to others. A Spirit-filled person will cooperate with Christ in working for others.

There are many ways to work for others. Our manner of life often has a powerful, silent influence. We can speak kind, encouraging words. We can offer assistance to someone in need. People who have the ability can tactfully help those who have health problems. At the appropriate time, we can speak about Christ and His love. When an individual is ready, we can present the special messages of God's Word.

The Constant Conflict With Our Fallen Natures

"The desires of the flesh are against the Spirit, and the desires of the Spirit are against the flesh; for these are opposed to each other, to prevent you from doing what you would" (Galatians 5:17, RSV).

Paul is speaking about the constant daily battle that is fought out in the life of every Christian. As believers in Christ, we have received the gift of righteousness because the Holy Spirit has come into our hearts (Romans 8:9, 10). But our weak, fallen humanity still remains. Paul was a totally dedicated Christian and a mighty preacher of the Word, but he knew that his only hope of overcoming the propensities of his fallen self was to rely totally on Jesus for strength. He wrote: "I keep under my body, and bring it into subjection: lest that by any means, when I have preached to others, I myself should be a castaway" (1 Corinthians 9:27).

"Paul's sanctification was a constant conflict with self. Said he: 'I die daily.' His will and his desires every day conflicted with duty and the will of God. Instead of following inclination, he did the will of God, however unpleasant and crucifying to his nature" (*Testimonies*, vol. 4, p. 299).

Notice that, even as a thoroughly born-again Christian, Paul had desires that needed to be subjugated. He was a fallen human being with biases to evil. But he did not give in to his fallen biases. He did God's will, whatever the sacrifice involved. Through the power of the indwelling Christ, Paul was able to overcome.

Romans 7:14-24 describes the struggle of the person who knows God's will but is having no success in doing it. The fallen nature is ruling and provoking the individual to commit the very sin that is despised. Romans 8:1-17 and Galatians 5:17, 18 describe the struggle experienced by all victorious Christians, who retain fallen humanity but who, through the power of the Holy Spirit, are successful in overcoming temptation.

Galatians 5:17 presents the conflict betwen natural inclinations and the will of the Holy Spirit in the life of every Christian. The last phrase may be translated, "so that you might not do whatever things you would wish." The Revised Standard Version renders it, "to prevent you from doing what you would." The point of the passage is not that the conflict between the Holy Spirit and the inclinations of the fallen self makes it impossible for us to do what is right. The point is that this conflict is designed by Satan to keep us from doing what we know is right. Paul hastens to add in the next verse that when we allow the Holy Spirit to control, we have victory.

Led by the Spirit

"If you are led by the Spirit you are not under the law" (Galatians 5:18, RSV).

Notice the context of this statement. Galatians 5:16 indicates that if we "walk by the Spirit" we will have victory over the desires of the flesh. Verse 17 presents the conflict that goes on in the life of every Christian. Verse 18 emphasizes the point of verse 16 in slightly different words. The phrase, "If you are led by the Spirit" (verse 18) describes the same experience as walking "by the Spirit" (verse 16). The person who does "not gratify the desires of the flesh" (verse 16) is the one who is "not under the law" (verse 18). In context, the point of verse 18 is that if the Spirit is in charge of our lives, we are not living in sin. We are not using the law as a means of salvation, nor are we breaking the law. By the power of the Holy Spirit we are enjoying spiritual victory.

The practical implications of that message are enormous. As believers in Christ who are walking "by the Spirit" we do not have to sin. Total victory is a very real possibility. Christ has made every provision for it. When we fall, the fault is entirely ours; we have failed to allow the Spirit to have His way in our lives; we have failed to grasp His power for victory. Total victory is Christ's ideal for His people.

"We can overcome. Yes; fully, entirely. Jesus died to make a way of escape for us, that we might overcome every fault, resist every temptation, and sit down at last with Him in His throne" (Our High Calling, p. 353).

"I saw that none could share the 'refreshing' unless they obtain the victory over every besetment, over pride, selfishness, love of the world, and over every wrong word and action. We should, therefore, be drawing nearer and nearer to the Lord and be earnestly seeking that preparation necessary to enable us to stand in the battle in the day of the Lord. Let all remember that God is holy and that none but holy beings can ever dwell in His presence" (Early Writings, p. 71).

The Works of the Flesh

Because the Galatian Christians had placed themselves under the law as the means of righteousness and salvation, they were vulnerable to the works of the flesh. There is no spiritual power in legalism. The attempt to "go it alone" without the grace of Christ is bound to result in failure. The evil one has a heyday with those who deny the significance of Calvary and imagine that they can conquer in their own strength.

The dilemma of the person who regards justification as a legal declaration in heaven but not a transformation of heart is equally troublesome. Such a person tends to feel that he is saved irrespective of the sins in his life. Justification is to him like an insurance policy that covers him, whatever the occasional lapses into the realm of the forbidden. Such an attitude is a false sense of security. There is no power in purely legal justification. The power comes through receiving the indwelling Christ by the presence of the Holy Spirit. That is Paul's point in the passage we are examining.

A legalist will inevitably fall into sin, whether he is a legalist because he attempts to keep the law in his own strength or because he accepts only half the Bible definition of justification. Such a person has no fortress against "the works of the flesh" itemized in Galatians 5:19-21.

Paul makes it perfectly clear that we are saved *from* our sins, not *in* our sins. "I warn you, as I warned you before, that those who do such things shall not inherit the kingdom of God" (Galatians 5:21, RSV). The Lord wants victors over sin in His heavenly kingdom. "Whatever is born of God *overcomes* the world; and this is the *victory* that overcomes the world, our faith" (1 John 5:4, RSV, italics supplied). Christianity is a message of spiritual victory, not a half-baked excuse for those who want the best of both worlds. "To him who overcomes, I will give the right to eat from the tree of life." "He who overcomes will not be hurt at all by the second death." "Him who overcomes I will make a pillar in the temple of my God." "To him who overcomes, I will give the right to sit with me on my throne" (Revelation 2:7, 11; 3:12, 21, NIV). Seven times in the message to the seven churches, Jesus upholds victory over sin as the qualification for heaven.

Praise the Lord, the justified believer, the born-again Christian who walks "in the Spirit" is an overcomer.

The Fruits of the Spirit

What beautiful qualities the Holy Spirit imparts to us! "Love, joy, peace, patience, kindness, goodness, faithfulness, gentleness, self-control; against such there is no law" (Galatians 5:22, 23, RSV). Paul made the same point when writing to the Romans by referring to justified believers as "slaves of righteousness" (Romans 6:18, RSV). They are *willing* slaves to the life of love and service that Jesus makes possible for them.

The power for this life comes from the Holy Spirit, who is daily received as He was initially received, into the heart of the humbly penitent believer.

"By constantly relying upon Christ as our personal Saviour, we shall grow up into Him in all things who is our head. . . . Christ is seeking to reproduce Himself in the hearts of men; and He does this through those who believe in Him. The object of the Christian life is fruit bearing—the reproduction of Christ's character in the believer, that it may be reproduced in others. . . .

"The graces of the Spirit will ripen in your character. Your faith will increase, your convictions deepen, your love be made perfect. More and more you will reflect the likeness of Christ in all that is pure, noble, and lovely. . . .

"Christ is waiting with longing desire for the manifestation of Himself in His church. When the character of Christ shall be perfectly reproduced in His people, then He will come to claim them as His own" (*Christ's Object Lessons*, pp. 67-69).

Summary

The fruitage in the lives of justified believers who have received and retain the presence of the Holy Spirit in their hearts is purity of purpose and motive, purity of speech and action, lovingkindness to friends and enemies, humility, gentleness, and unobtrusiveness. Jesus is this kind of person, and He wants us to reflect His character.

Chapter 13
Reaping Time

Galatians 6:1-18

Paul completes his epistle to the Galatians by writing of the reward for saved, loving Christians. As always, Jesus is the example. His life of service, His patience with the erring, His willingness to stoop to lift a fallen soul, and His forgiveness of His enemies provide the pattern for our lives. Even though a reward is promised, the motive for our service is not the reward. The joy of seeing others redeemed, delivered from the misery of sin by being introduced to the Saviour of the world, is the reward for Christ's faithful followers. Heaven will be a perfect place for a perfected people; the real joy will be personal association with Jesus and with those who are there because of our humble witness.

A Spirit of Gentleness

"Brothers, if someone is caught in a sin, you who are spiritual should restore him gently. But watch yourself, or you also may be tempted" (Galatians 6:1, NIV). How easy it is to condemn our fellow church members who fall into sin! We tend to feel somewhat more righteous than others when we hear of someone else's failure. We tend to compare the fallen church member or minister with ourselves and conclude that he or she is deserving of discipline and punishment. This pharisaical attitude was obnoxious to Jesus. He said, "Judge not, that ye be not judged. For with what judgment ye judge, ye shall be judged: and with what measure ye mete, it shall be measured to you again" (Matthew 7:1, 2).

An *objective* look at others may reveal in stark reality their terrible weakness and sin. But it is not so easy to be as objective about our own sins. "Why beholdest thou the mote that is in thy brother's eye, but considerest not the beam that is in thine own eye?" (Matthew 7:3).

The offending party is often subjected to social ostracism, nasty letters, harsh criticism, and the silent treatment. It is always more comfortable to totally ignore a condemned sinner than to "stain one's garments" by speaking to him or her, offering a friendly smile, a warm handshake, and an encouraging word. If Jesus had treated the woman taken in adultery or Mary Magdalene or Peter in the manner in which we sometimes treat sinners in our churches, we would be deprived of some of the most beautiful stories in the gospel record, and those poor sinners would be deprived of eternal life.

Harsh rebuke rarely results in the saving of a soul. The sinner often knows his need. Kindness, forgiveness, and understanding are hard to resist; they produce positive results.

"If Christ is in you 'the hope of glory,' you will have no disposition to watch others, to expose their errors. Instead of seeking to accuse and condemn, it will be your object to help, to bless, and to save. In dealing with those who are in error, you will heed the injunction, Consider 'thyself, lest thou also be tempted.' Galatians 6:1. You will call to mind the many times you have erred and how hard it was to find the right way when you had once left it. You will not push your brother into greater darkness, but with a heart full of pity will tell him of his danger" (*Thoughts From the Mount of Blessing*, p. 128).

"Look to yourself, lest you too be tempted" (Galatians 6:1, RSV). A humble awareness of our own weaknesses and of Christ's wonderful mercy in saving us from ruin will make us ever ready to forgive the fallen, and to do everything we can to reinstate them. To remember people's sins after they have repented and Jesus has forgiven them is to disqualify oneself for forgiveness (see Matthew 18:21-35).

"He who looks often upon the cross of Calvary, remembering that his sins placed the Saviour there, will never try to estimate the degree of his guilt in comparison with that of others. He will not climb upon the judgment seat to bring accusation against another. There can be no spirit of criticism or self-exaltation on the part of those who walk in the shadow of Calvary's cross" (*Thoughts From the Mount of Blessing*, p. 128).

Bearing One Another's Burdens

"Bear one another's burdens, and so fulfil the law of Christ" (Galatians 6:2, RSV). Jesus' teaching regarding treatment of our faulty brethren and sisters was obviously the basis of Paul's teaching. Jesus said that the "golden rule" (see Matthew 7:12) summarizes the message of Scripture ("the law and the prophets"). This rule is to govern our attitudes to enemies, as well as to friends (see Matthew 5:43-48). Human relationships are probably the most complicating factor in church life. The only way to achieve good fellowship and unity of spirit is to follow the counsel of Jesus.

Only a willingly blind person could fail to recognize the fearful burdens that many people are carrying. Some are struggling against secret sin that is so habitual and ingrained that they hold out little hope for themselves. But they must not despair; we must inspire them to rely more fully on Jesus for the victory. Others are experiencing hurtful family problems of one kind or another. Still others are battling with health problems or financial problems. There are some very lonely people in our churches who are too retiring in disposition to make close friends, but who crave love and acceptance. And there are still others who are grieving the loss of a family member or a friend.

Whatever the problem, we can at least show kindness and loving concern for the one who is struggling and suffering. At the end of one of my sermons at a camp meeting some years ago I gave an invitation for those who would like to surrender to Christ to come forward so that I could pray with them. One young man came forward and waited quite a long time while I talked with the people who pressed around me. He told me that he had committed a terrible sin and had been disfellowshiped by his church. I said, "Brother, the Lord will forgive you and receive you back as one of His children." He replied, "Oh, yes, I know Jesus forgives me, but I don't think the church members will."

What a tragic indictment of us as Christians! Christ can forgive and ignore past failures, but we cannot. Even if the brother were wrong in his evaluation of the church members, what a tragedy that he should have received that impression! It is our responsibility to reassure, to win, to impart new hope and confidence to those overwhelmed with sorrow for sins.

The Dangers of Self-Confidence

Perhaps the main reason we tend to ignore the burdens of those around us and look with disdain upon sinners is that, as we compare ourselves with them, we appear to be superior in holiness. Paul warns us: "If any one thinks he is something, when he is nothing, he deceives himself" (Galatians 6:3, RSV). Comparing ourselves with others is bound to result in distorted judgment (see verse 4). We must take a long, hard, objective look at our own attitudes and habits, comparing ourselves with Jesus and allowing Him to make us like Himself (see Luke 14:7-11; Romans 12:3; 1 Corinthians 8:2).

"In self-love, self-exaltation, and pride there is great weakness; but in humility there is great strength. Our true dignity is not maintained when we think most of ourselves, but when God is in all our thoughts and our hearts are all aglow with love to our Redeemer and love to our fellow men. Simplicity of character and lowliness of heart will give happiness, while self-conceit will bring discontent, repining, and continual disappointment. It is learning to think less of ourselves and more of making others happy that will bring to us divine strength" (*Testimonies*, vol. 3, p. 476).

"Do not be deceived; God is not mocked, for whatever a man sows, that he will also reap. For he who sows to his own flesh will from the flesh reap corruption; but he who sows to the Spirit will from the Spirit reap eternal life" (Galatians 6:7, 8, RSV).

In the context of the epistle to the Galatians, sowing to the Spirit is receiving justification. As we begin with the Spirit (see Galatians 3:3), and walk daily by the Spirit (see Galatians 5:16, 18) we have peace with God (see Romans 5:1), the love of God reigning in our hearts (see Romans 5:5), and the assurance of eternal life (see John 3:36; 1 John 5:11-13).

Sowing to the flesh is the opposite experience. It involves rejection of justification (the new-birth experience) and all the tragedies and evils that result. In place of the Holy Spirit, the devil is the master of the life; selfishness reigns supreme, and the works of the flesh are paramount (see Romans 5:19-21). The apostle Paul sadly wrote the epitaph of those who unrepentantly sow to the flesh: "Their end is destruction" (Philippians 3:19, RSV).

Those who sow to the Spirit do "not grow weary in well-doing, for in due season we shall reap, if we do not lose heart" (Galatians 6:9, RSV). The reaping time is the coming of Jesus: "The harvest is the end of the world" (Matthew 13:39). "Then shall the righteous shine forth as the sun in the kingdom of their Father" (verse 43). The experience of justification, maintained and perpetuated, empowers us to render loving service to others and culminates in the eternal joys of the heavenly kingdom. "So then, as we have opportunity, let us do good to all men, and especially to those who are of the household of faith" (Galatians 6:10, RSV).

Glory in the Cross

Paul wrote the final sentences of his epistle with his characteristic large handwriting (see Galatians 6:11). Because he was partially blind (see Galatians 4:15), he usually wrote by dictating his letters to a secretary. To give final authenticity to the letter, he added a postscript in his own handwriting.

To bring the Galatians back to the central burden of his epistle, Paul reminded them of the futility of practicing circumcision as a religious ritual (see Galatians 6:12, 13). He reminded them that the motives of the legalists who wanted them to be circumcised were very much open to question. By practicing circumcision, they sought to avoid the inevitable persecution that they would receive from orthodox Jews. The legalists were looking for a following, seeking disciples, coveting religious recognition, and ignoring the cross of Christ.

Paul sought to bring the Galatians back to the realities of victorious Christian living. "Far be it from me to glory except in the cross of our Lord Jesus Christ, by which the world has been crucified to me, and I to the world. For neither circumcision counts for anything, nor uncircumcision, but a new creation" (Galatians 6:14, 15, RSV).

Our hope centers in the cross of Christ. As He died *for* our sin, so we must die *to* our sin (see Romans 6:5-8). As He rose the victor over sin and death, so we must rise to newness of life in Him. As He overcame by total reliance upon His Father, so we must depend upon Him for deliverance from the power of evil. "He who conquers, I will grant him to sit with me on my throne, as I myself conquered and sat down with my Father on his throne" (Revelation 3:21, RSV).

"God will accept only those who are determined to aim high. He places every human agent under obligation to do his best. Moral perfection is required of all. Never should we lower the standard of righteousness in order to accommodate inherited or cultivated tendencies to wrongdoing. We need to understand that imperfection of character is sin. All righteous attributes of character dwell in God as a perfect, harmonious whole, and every one who receives Christ as a personal Saviour is privileged to possess these attributes" (*Christ's Object Lessons*, p. 330).

The cross renders possible "a new creation" in our hearts. In place of moral and spiritual degradation, there is purity and love. In place of hopeless discontent with our own attitudes and with the circumstances of our lives, there is peace of mind, satisfaction in service, and joy in Christian fellowship. In place of habitual sin, there is habitual victory. In place of Satan's tyrannical rule, there is the benevolent reign of the Holy Spirit. Our heartfelt praise is that of the apostle Paul: "For to me to live is Christ" (Philippians 1:21).

"The grace of our Lord Jesus Christ be with your spirit. Amen" (Galatians 6:18).